Worship Beyond Nationalism

Worship Beyond Nationalism

Practicing the Reign of God

ROB HEWELL

WIPF & STOCK · Eugene, Oregon

WORSHIP BEYOND NATIONALISM
Practicing the Reign of God

Wipf & Stock
An Imprint of Wipf and Stock Publishers
199 W. 8th Ave., Suite 3
Eugene, OR 97401
www.wipfandstock.com

ISBN 13: 978-61097-468-4

Manufactured in the U.S.A.

Some concepts in this book appeared in "Faithful Worship" by Rob Hewell in *The Minister's Manual 2010 Edition*, Edited by Lee McGlone, copyright © 2009, Lee McGlone. Reprinted with the permission of John Wiley & Sons, Inc.

To Cyndy
—the love of my life

-and-

For Christ's followers in all times and places
whose affections, allegiance, and actions
manifest faithfulness in living out
the grand liturgy of the eternal kingdom:
"love the Lord your God
with all your heart,
and with all your soul,
and with all your mind,
and with all your strength." and
"love your neighbour as yourself."

—MARK 12:30–31 (NRSV)

Contents

Foreword

OUR DEEPEST loyalties live next to each other in the depths of our soul. They are few in number, only two or three, yet they form the center of our being. Our deepest loyalties constitute the "hills we would die on." For many American Christians these loyalties are God, country, and family. Perhaps there was a time when they could be listed by priority: 1. God, 2. Country, 3. Family, with the claim that in that order, none would suffer. Times have changed and the three deepest loyalties seem to have been rearranged, resting now side by side on the same plane, any one of the three available to come to the fore of thought and action as "loyalty number one," according to circumstance. The shift is profound in its implications. Exodus 20:1–8 shouts at the shift, but to no avail. The cries of the commandment are overpowered by the din of 9/11 scandalization, political division, and calls to reestablish a Constantinian Christian America. American flags are posted in the worship sanctuaries of "Church Families" across the United States, with the congregations' common national enemies and issues providing at least as much inspiration as is their common loving Lord. Rob Hewell has observed these things and with this book speaks in a calm, clear, rational voice that will surely pierce the continuous noise of partisan rhetoric by its sheer contrast to blinded eyes, hoarse voices, and frightened minds.

It must be acknowledged that responsible patriotism is the duty of all citizens, even Christian citizens. At its root, the word patriotism simply refers to one's love for or loyalty to their homeland. We are called to love God supremely, but we are not called to love God exclusively. So there is room for patriotism in the heart and life of a Christian. Borrowing from a discussion of taxes, we are admonished to give to Caesar the things that are Caesar's and to God the things that are God's. However, we are called to worship God exclusively (again, Exodus 20). Christian worship cannot and will not abide anything that even remotely resembles the worship of another god. Here is the danger of the three loyalties being stored on the "same shelf" in the Christian's deepest heart. They can become entangled at the call to worship.

Responsible patriotism is a communal force focused on the welfare and betterment of each other and of humankind in general. It can easily be at home in the Christian heart, resonating with the call to ministry in the name of Jesus, but it cannot and would not be the focus of Christian worship. Nationalism, as opposed to patriotism, is the most ugly and destructive force on our planet and in human history. Somewhere in the migration from patriotism to nationalism, exclusivity and triumphalism enter the picture and the heart. For Christians there can be no participation in nationalism; this is especially true in the context of worship. Endorsing nationalism, especially the sort that blindly stumbles into the sanctuary and considers itself to be the equivalent of worship, can only be categorized as idolatry. Nationalistic worship and civil religion are signs of disillusionment with the gospel, disappointment with the Creator, respectful disgust with the teachings of Jesus, and disconnect from the Holy Spirit. Nationalism is patriotism that has grown impatient with, even frightened of, the Kingdom of God's orientation of heart and mind.

For many Christians, patriotism is seen as the one acceptable pride that a Christ-follower may politely possess and exhibit. At best, these believers bring their patriotism into worship so that it might undergo purification and divine validation, so that it might be returned to proper perspective. In that regard, one might say that patriotism could rightly bow before the Master who heals and blesses, who receives confession and forgives. But patriotism that stands tall in the place and context of Christian worship, refusing to bow its knee and retire its colors, has already morphed into nationalism. Nothing should cause the worshiper or the liturgy to declare in word, deed, or symbol an exclusivity or triumphalism that the Christ being worshiped will not own. Jesus will not bless our pride, nor will pride bow its heart.

Disturbingly, a poem comes to mind: W.B. Yeats' *The Second Coming*. Only three lines deep into his insight Yeats declares that "Things fall apart; the centre cannot hold." Nationalistic worship is a sign that a nation's patriotism is suffering division and is falling apart, clinging to Christian worship to stop, or at least slow, the deterioration. Nationalism moves beyond the prayer of 2 Chronicles 7:14 and calls on the nation to save Christianity. Nationalistic worship is a sign that within that nation's culture and identity, the declared center, Christianity, cannot hold in its Christ-following form. In other words, Jesus refuses to be an American and Uncle Sam cannot be Messiah. Things fall apart. Therefore, if Christianity is to be reestablished as the center of the culturally and religiously diverse nation the United States has inevitably become, it must be redefined, divorced and diluted from "Christ-following" of the gospel order. Nationalistic worship's Christianity, in our world, must be redefined as "not Muslim."

We have never said that one must first become a Christian to become a U.S. citizen. Let us not, then, declare that one must first become an American (and of a particular political sort) to become a worshiper of Christ.

Pulses race and fears run rampant at such thoughts and words and debate. Under the influence of fear, we call upon the three deep loyalties to rise up as one, sacrificing family and Christianity in defense and protection of our nation. On-going discussions of a good and strong nation's responsibility in an evil and cruel world enter the sanctuary no longer as prayers for guidance, but now as prayers for victory. The blood stains of the cross and the red stripes of the flag blur. We determine that in times like ours Jesus' peace must wait until Christmas, Jesus' victory must wait until Easter, and Jesus' dying for enemies must wait until the second advent.

Perhaps freedom of worship, even Christian worship, in the United States has finally met the oppressor who would imprison it. It wasn't communism after all. It is well intentioned loyalty combined with un-checked fear, morphing into incipient idolatry. No dictator has sent armed troops into our sanctuaries and the drifting can be reversed by means of repentance. But where are the voices of the prophets? Where is Rabbi Friedman's "nonanxious presence"? Where are the pastors who will lead us with courage through the maze of our dual citizenship in the kingdoms of Heaven and earth?

Enough sidestepping and polite walking away, enough of silence in the name of differences of opinion and taste, enough simultaneous shouting; Rob Hewell has shown up with the Bible (all of it) in his hand and "Jesus is Lord" (all the time) in his heart and mind. There is clear thinking here; unusual, hopeful, clear thinking. Further, there is hope to be found in the hearts of Christian patriots in America who really do want to worship aright the one true God, even though they have been caught up in the current rage and fury, and even though to worship God without a flag seems strangely vulnerable and un-American. The hope lies in clear-minded study of scripture, earnest and humble prayer, and worship that bows low enough before God to rise above 24/7 televised shouting matches, grief for a lost "Christian America" past (real and imagined), and fear of a reordered future. One last thought: The absence of the flag in worship is not enough. It must be explained by the presence of the cross.

Terry W. York
George W. Truett Theological Seminary
Baylor University
Waco, Texas
Fall, 2011

Introduction

LISTEN TO the conversations at just about any gathering of Christians, regardless of the purpose for the gathering, and at some point the topic of worship is likely to come up. There is plenty of fuel for those moments, since worship is considered to be so central to our understanding of faith and life and there are so many dimensions to be considered. It is a much-studied facet of the church's internal atmosphere and external identity. Any review of pertinent websites or available titles from online or on-the-shelf suppliers affirms that reality. The discussion of worship nears the level of sport in many quarters of Christianity.

While everyone seems to have an opinion as to what worship is or is not, or a preference for how it should be expressed, one truth seems evident: worship is in danger of being misunderstood or misappropriated. If worship truly is in any danger, it is so at least partially because of our readiness to be satisfied far too quickly with something that seems suitable even though it may not be complete or anywhere near correct.

There is no attempt here to get at the full range of possible perilous misunderstandings or misappropriations; the possibilities are far too numerous. This book does, however, seek to provide some perspective on one such possibility: to offer clarity regarding worship in light of the politics of God's reign in Christ. In other words, this book is about worship as a political act.

Faithfulness to the triune God in worship is in and of itself a precarious proposition since it challenges our affections and loyalties for all things temporal and worldly. Such faithfulness is at stake on this count. A distinct word on this matter is crucial if confusions and misperceptions are to be minimized—if not avoided altogether.

Getting at this subject adequately requires some grasp of concepts regarding the church's witness and history, the gospel, worship in its many dimensions, and culture. It also requires some understanding of the way power is leveraged for the strength and sustenance of nation-states and partisan political entities, and how religion, and even the church and its symbols and narrative, are sometimes used (and even abused) for those ends. Drawing these concepts into the same discussion with the nature of worship necessitates caution, finesse, nuance, and no small amount of courage.

Indeed, the interrelatedness of politics and religion is a timely subject in our world, particularly in the United States (U.S.), and specifically among evangelical Christians in this country. Calls for specifying the U.S. as a Christian nation in some quarters, matched by calls for the firm separation of church and state in others, enjoy daily media exposure. Without a doubt, the nation's founding documents—definitely political in their own right—afford Christians the freedom to worship freely and openly. The same freedom is cast to groups and persons who choose other religious persuasions, or who prefer to ignore or even defame religious practice altogether. In theory at least, all faith or faithless expressions have equal opportunity to participate in the broader society.

Although lacking formal terminological cachet in America's founding documents, the separation of church and state is the customary defining boundary between the two institutions. It is valuable and worth sustaining, and is deeply embedded in the doctrinal DNA in many quarters of evangelicalism. It is a functional dichotomy, however, belying an arguably weightier reality—politics and religion entwine enthusiastically in the open marketplace of pluralist ideologies. The passions stirred by each become hard-to-resist compelling forces, drawing each toward the other with magnetic abandon.

From its earliest inception, this nation's patriotic demeanor has readily invoked a religious tenor. The story of national essence is emboldened by what is generally accepted as divine providence in its founding and flourishing. No doubt nationalism is a powerful force, propelling the U.S. through its headiest days while sustaining it through its darkest nights. Even further, the tendency toward America's well-intended hegemony has generally fostered a forceful partisan political practice within virtually all of its spheres of influence.

Evangelicalism's penchant for institution building is a reflection of its participation in Christendom in general and in American culture in particular. The church as institution in the U.S. has been well schooled in such tendencies, seeking to exercise its will by trading on the influences of partisan clout. Arguably, these influences generally lack deep consonance with the gospel of Jesus Christ. While not always overtly anti-gospel, they nonetheless give ultimate priority to the fitness and maintenance of the American statist agenda. Even when components of this nationalized agenda appear on the surface to be compatible with biblical mandates, jingoistic intent tends to insist on the subjugation of the gospel to that intent. It is no stretch to suggest that these dynamics are at least partially responsible for the compromise of faithfulness in worship among evangelical congregations within the American experience.

When nationalism propagates itself through a cross-pollination of the stories, symbols, and celebrations of religious groups with the nation-state, the stage is set for a national history bearing the character of sacrosanct myth. The stage is also set for confusion within the life of the church. Such civil religious activity is likely to create dissonance for Christ's followers between what they understand to be biblical and what civil religion supports as religiously valid.

I am certainly not alone in a deepening conviction that the faithfulness of communal worship in the evangelical tradition in

America has been compromised in various ways, this lack of clarity about politics being just one concern. The dilemma might be stated this way: *How is it possible for Christ's followers to worship faithfully in a nationalistic environment where religion and politics enjoy a vigorous affiliation while the separation of church and state is celebrated as the standard for the relationship between nation and faith?*

No doubt religion in the U.S. exists in a highly-charged political environment. Political activity is certainly a necessary element of civilized society. Being political is part and parcel of American citizenship—no less for Christians who live in this country than for anyone else. Turning a collective back on political activity is a tempting option. Yet leaving politicality to a realm outside of faith is unsatisfactory for various reasons, not the least would be the danger of diminishing the fullness of the gospel of Jesus Christ.

Absent an appropriate balancing influence, the political character of the life, teachings, and ministry of Christ falls too easily into worldly maneuvers that are inconsistent with biblical faith. (So also the witness of Christ's followers.) The kingdom of God exists in, but not of, this world and has political responsibilities that are yet distinct from the machinations of this world. It is my conviction that the necessary balancing influence for the political character of God's reign in Christ is liturgical. In spite of modernity's ability to deftly separate elements of life into sacred and secular dominions, what appears to be two—political and liturgical—may indeed be more nearly one in the economy of the kingdom of heaven.

There are political implications for faithfulness in Christian worship. To deny that is to diminish the truth about worship. The challenge lies in subtlety, at times, for what is added to worship that may be questionable, but more frequently for what is not sufficiently manifest. Worship among evangelicals in the U.S. is rarely flagrantly nationalistic on a weekly basis. Yet is it often enough unclear about which—or *whose*—politics it favors, those of Caesar or those of God revealed in the story of ancient Israel and in the person of Jesus Christ.

Jesus was clear in his pronouncements about the reign of God. These truths were not always easily understood by those who walked with Jesus and heard his teachings. Even today truths about God's kingdom require an entirely dissimilar orientation to reality than the world has always assumed as correct. The followers of Jesus must be obvious in living as witnesses to the reign of God. Doing so is somewhat complicated for Christians in America, a country whose national ethos-myth is steeped in a blatant worldly exercise of power within its own borders as well as on the global stage. Followers of Jesus have a citizenship that transcends and supersedes all earthly loyalties. Faithful worship makes this distinction clear.

It is not enough to simply inquire about the political character of worship. This work would be incomplete without some regard for the witness that faithful worshipers bear into this world. That witness calls for service, humility, and a conviction that God has come in Christ to be Lord of all creation, not confined to one realm or another. The church exists for the glory of God and for the sake of the world. Therefore, the quality of worship among Christians has a direct influence on the value of their witness in the world. The measure of encounters with the world will be revealed by the depth and richness of encounters with God in worship.

Faithfulness to triune God in worship is crucial for navigating such challenges encountered by congregations as they seek to live their witness into the world through actions that proclaim the reign of God. It must give substance to our understanding of Christ's injunctions to his followers who are to be salt and light in the world without being of the world. Herein is a dynamic rubric for interpreting the dimensions, elements, and acts of worship in light of God's politics, which represent a reign already begun but not yet fully revealed.

Worship Beyond Nationalism is an exploration of topics identified in this Introduction. It is not intended to be an overarching volume on worship *per se*. The focus is intentionally narrow in scope. No doubt there are many related topics not addressed here. What the reader will encounter in these pages is probably more descriptive than prescriptive—more *consider this* than *do this*. The thoughts presented in these pages will probably raise as many questions as they answer. While I have sought to write confidently about these matters, there is no attempt to declare these to be complete or final words on any of them. My purpose is to be faithful with concepts as I have come to understand them, and to foster significant conversations within the church regarding its worship and witness.

The terms *world* and *worldly* will appear frequently throughout *Worship Beyond Nationalism*. In this context, it should be understood to refer to the social, cultural, spiritual, and political paradigms present in human experience in any given age in history. In general the term will be used to refer to ways of life that are distinct from the living witness of Christians—explicitly identified as Christ's followers representing faithfulness to God in worship, the church's identity as the body of Christ, and the church's Christ-formed agency on behalf of God's kingdom.

Faithful worship requires absolute clarity about the worship of God in Christ. It properly orients Christ's followers to the politics of God's reign rather than those of worldly Caesars, and shapes the church for liturgical participation in *missio Dei*. It is precisely as the people of God become a holy nation and a royal priesthood that they indeed become church in the fullest, most biblical sense.

Worship Beyond Nationalism explores faithful worship as a political act by which the church declares allegiance to God in Christ rather than to any worldly empires. Faithful worship enables congregations to enact the reality of God's kingdom and to embody the gospel for the glory of God and for the sake of the world.

1

Liturgy of the Kingdom

THE INCARNATION of God in Christ Jesus was tangible evidence of the in-breaking of God's kingdom, an arrival of the most radical sort. God's appearance in Christ was historically organic, expressed in a specific season of human history, in a particular geography with deliberate ethnic imprimatur. Yet the coming of this transcendent kingdom and its definitive Sovereign was also historically dynamic. It encompassed long seasons of prophetic anticipation, was revealed in Christ's personhood through sometimes confusing parables and numinous miracles, and pointed to an eschatological realization.

The coming of God in Christ was certainly an act of grace and mercy without equal on the part of a holy and loving God. That does not, however, mitigate the fact that it was also an enormous provocation designed to serve notice to all of creation that the Creator was wholly committed to redemption and re-creation. When taken at face value, the message of Christ's life, teaching, and ministry brings the world face to face with the eternal kingdom of love. It is this kingdom, and the worship of this kingdom's Sovereign, that require our attention in these pages.

Scripture is clear that the sovereignty of God's reign in Christ extends to the fullest reaches of life and existence. No realm of creation is exempt—including the political arena. The apostle Paul signaled this truth when he wrote that Christ "is the image of the invisible God" and "in him all things in heaven and earth were

1

created, things visible and invisible, whether *thrones* or *dominions* or *rulers* or *powers*—all things have been created through him and for him" (emphasis mine).[1] In Christ "the whole fullness of deity dwells bodily" and he "*is the head of every ruler and authority*" and "*He disarmed the rulers and authorities and made a public example of them, triumphing over them*" (emphasis mine).[2] Again, Paul wrote regarding "the immeasurable greatness of [God's] power for us who believe." This is the very power that worked in Christ who is not only resurrected from the dead but has ascended to God's right hand in the heavenly places. It is the glorious Father who "has put all things under [Christ's] feet and has made him the head over all things for the church, which is his body, the fullness of him who fills all in all."[3] The obvious force of God's sovereignty invested in Christ is a bold statement of God's political initiative.

To say such things about anyone cuts against the grain of the world's self-affirming confidence in its own ways and wisdom. For those things to be said of Jesus Christ as identified in the biblical narrative is an offense of even greater magnitude. Jesus of Nazareth claimed not only to be the Son of God, but also claimed to be one with God. The sting of such boldness cost Jesus Christ his human life. The dare to risk, however, creates the tension by which the gospel wounds the world for the sake of the world's healing. So it is that it could be said that "Jesus Christ was the supreme divine intrusion into the world's settled arrangements."[4]

Kingdom was not an unfamiliar concept among first century Jews. They were certainly well-steeped in the triumph and tragedy of their own national existence. The nation's encounters with a multitude of other kingdoms and empires were the essence of lore. The practice of remembrance recalled an exodus of massive proportions: a departure from life in one oppressive kingdom, only

1. Col 1:15–16.
2. Col 2:9b, 10b, 15.
3. Eph 1:19–20, 22–23.
4. Hauerwas and Willimon, *Resident Aliens*, 51.

to encounter numerous others on their way to a land promised by the God of Jacob, and a home for the descendants of Joseph who were the great nation of promise to Abram. The cumulative reality for ancient Israel was one of struggle for identity and independence. Their current status, as underlings in the powerful and ever-present Roman imperium, was a daily reminder of a unique ethnic and religious heritage to which they could give only partial expression. Their place in the world was not entirely their own.

Into this environment of incomplete dominion came John, the one known as the baptizer, proclaiming the nearness of the kingdom of heaven. His message was not original. Isaiah had predicted that a proclaimer would come, one who would precede a promised Messiah. The kingdom to be established by this Messiah would be an eternal one, for which failure was not a possibility. Accustomed to less successful ventures in creating and sustaining dominion, the kings and people of Judah looked forward to a kingdom without fail. Some seven hundred years or so later the post-Isaiah Israelites who encountered John's message were still hoping for Messiah, though with a skewed character. Since the commencement of Roman rule six decades earlier, Jewish expectations for Messiah had taken a decidedly nationalistic turn with nearly unqualified inclination to a worldly means-to-an-end. Those expectations quite missed the point of the prophet's inimitable message.

The people who heard John's statements and responded to his plea for repentance and baptism were yet clueless about the true nearness of heaven's kingdom. The baptizer's message made it clear he himself was not the promised one of Israel. There was another coming that would transcend John's own identity as messenger. John's audience was witnessing the arrival of the kingdom, if they would but discern its manifestation among them. The arrival of the long-awaited Messiah was shocking, not because of its force but for its lack of force in worldly terms.

Jesus Christ's own declarations regarding the kingdom of God were as numerous as they were enigmatic. Christ was constantly and pointedly drawing attention to the kingdom of God. No doubt the expectations of his hearers were culturally formed. Their hope for a warrior-king, much in the model of David, was deep-set and constantly nurtured. These expectations were clearly evident as Jesus approached Jerusalem days before his execution as the people shouted, "Blessed is the coming kingdom of our ancestor David!"[5] To be sure, Jesus' own lineage was traceable to mighty king David. Yet Jesus clearly proclaimed the kingdom of heaven—that of his Father God—not the rule of David. The misunderstanding represented by this praiseful acclamation was telling. Their hope was in the true Messiah, yet their goals were inconsistent with his aims of faithfulness to his Father's will.

This much they knew: freedom would come at a price. All that was lacking was someone willing to accept the mantle of leading the uprising, one surely to signal a return to sovereignty over their own affairs. This person would also assume enormous risk, a dare most were generally unwilling to take. Was it not the word of the LORD God through the prophets that Messiah would come? Jesus Christ resisted the efforts of the Jews to cast him into their agenda, steadfastly preferring the agenda of his Father's kingdom.

It would be unwise to overlook the second Testament's focus on the kingdom of God. The term *kingdom* appears more than 160 times in the New Testament. It is understood to refer to a realm in which a particular king reigns. It is inclusive of the authority and sovereignty exercised by and fully vested in the ruler. A majority of the uses of three Greek forms[6] are credited to Jesus Christ in referring to his Father's kingdom, identified interchangeably as the kingdom of God or the kingdom of heaven. The terms are also used by Luke, Paul, John, and the writer of the book of Hebrews.

---

5. Mark 11:10.

6. The New Testament uses the Greek βασιλεία, βασιλείαν and βασιλείας.

The language reveals clear pronouncements about the impending arrival, present reality, and future fulfillment of God's kingdom.

The kingdom of heaven was declared to be imminent in the words of John the baptizer, "Repent, for the kingdom of heaven has come near," and of Jesus himself, "As you go, proclaim the good news, 'The kingdom of heaven has come near.'"[7] In other instances, the original language delivers news of the kingdom as being present. Jesus persistently spoke of the kingdom as a present reality: "Blessed are those who are persecuted for righteousness' sake, for theirs is the kingdom of heaven" and "the kingdom of God is among you" and "My kingdom is not from this world."[8] In the first instance, Jesus is teaching about blessedness among those who seek and live humbly. Jesus offers the second in response to the Pharisees' inquiry about the arrival of this kingdom. The third comes in response to Pilate's question about Jesus' kingship. While there was a sense in which the kingdom was in existence before their very eyes, Jesus' audiences were many times either unable or unwilling to see it. The kingdom of God was not new, yet it was newly near.

Jesus' encounter with the chief priests and elders in the temple is instructive as well. At the conclusion of a parable regarding wicked tenants—itself a pointed accusation of the elders and priests—Jesus declares, "the kingdom of God will be taken away from you and given to a people that produces the fruits of the kingdom."[9] The suggestion here is that something cannot be taken away unless it is first available to the persons from whom it is to be taken.

7. Matt 3:2 and 10:7 respectively. In these instances the Greek verb ἤγγικεν is from ἐγγίζω and is rendered *to make near* or *to come near*, or most properly *has drawn close*.

8. In order, Matt 5:10, Luke 17:21b, and John 18.36a. In these examples, the word *is* is translated from the Greek ἐστί and rendered as *are, belong, call, come,* or *consist*; it is in the third person singular present indicative of εἰμί, the verb meaning *I am*, or *exist*.

9. Matt 21:43.

The biblical narrative indicates that on the Passover night prior to Jesus' arrest, he blessed bread and cup, encouraging his disciples to eat and drink with new understanding of what it means to be in covenant with God. He then astounded them by saying he would drink the fruit of the vine with them next in the kingdom of his Father—and not until then.[10] Here Jesus invests the kingdom with a discernible futurity, a promise of fulfillment those present in that gathering could scarcely comprehend in that moment.

Jesus' life, ministry, and teachings were, among many things, political. The politicality represented in Christ is an accurate reflection of the reign of God, and the politics of this reign are distinct from all worldly politics. If, indeed, all things were created through Christ and for Christ, then the most direct path into the kingdom of heaven is through Christ himself. God's reign in Christ is the kingdom of God.

Jesus Christ was, indeed, the full embodiment of this new kingdom. In fact, some early church fathers referred to Jesus as *autobasileia*—the "Kingdom in himself." By extending the force of Paul's descriptions of Christ in his epistles to the Ephesians and Colossians, that very assertion is appropriate: "For [Christ] is the King of the heavens, and as He is absolute Wisdom and absolute Righteousness and absolute Truth, is He not so also absolute Kingdom? . . . if you enquire into the meaning of the words, 'Theirs is the kingdom of heaven,' you may say that Christ is theirs in so far as He is absolute Kingdom."[11]

Such striking language is evident in contemporaneous thought as well, given expression from another quarter of the Christian faith: "Jesus himself is the Kingdom; the Kingdom is not a thing, it is not a geographical dominion like worldly kingdoms. It is a person; it is he. On this interpretation, the term 'Kingdom of God' is itself a veiled Christology. By the way in which he speaks of

---

10. Matt 26:29, Luke 22:18, and Mark 14:25. In Matt and Mark, the phrase ἕως τῆς ἡμέρας—*until the day* is the operative qualifier.

11. Origen, *Commentary on the Gospel of Matthew.*

the Kingdom of God, Jesus leads men to realize the overwhelming fact that in him God himself is present among them, that he is God's presence."[12]

To be sure, Jesus Christ lived among humankind in a specific time and place. Yet the primary context in which he did what he did and said what he said was not a Jewish society struggling to survive under first-century Roman rule. The primary context of his birth, every encounter, conversation, miracle, and even his crucifixion, resurrection, and ascension was the kingdom of God. Christ literally inaugurated life in this new kingdom in his very self. Hence for Christ's followers to be in Christ and to obey the commands of Christ is to be in the kingdom.

The incarnation of God in Christ revealed the kingdom of God to the world. What is difficult to accept, however, is that the purpose of the incarnation was not to prove the kingdom of God was relevant to the world. If that was truly the purpose of the incarnation, one could argue that the incarnation was a failure. Isaiah's prophecy regarding Messiah became all too tragically true; the One who would be "despised and rejected" and "oppressed, and . . . afflicted . . . like a lamb that is led to the slaughter"[13] was not even welcomed by those of his own ethnic heritage.[14]

During his earthly life Jesus Christ was questioned regularly, often by persons allied with groups attempting to catch him in some heretical or treasonous act. He had a propensity for responding to them in ways that curtailed their capacity to entrap him. At every turn, Jesus was faithfully representing the perspective of the reign of God. It was clear that by God's presence in Christ, God's reign was breaking into the world, yet it was not of the world. Jesus' responses were rarely intended to confuse, yet they continually confounded the world's ways. His answers constantly challenged the assumptions of the inquisitors. He also challenged their pre-

12. Benedict XVI, *Jesus of Nazareth*, 49.
13. Isa 53:3a, 7a.
14. John 1:11.

7

sumptions about their prerogative in deciding what was right and what was true.

In his gospel narrative, Matthew records a monumental conversation, one between Jesus and a group of Pharisees.[15] A scribe asked Jesus, "Which commandment in the law is the greatest?" They were seeking to test Jesus. It did not occur to them that they, like so many others, were offering Christ the opportunity to speak truth almost beyond their willingness (if not their ability) to understand. The first commandment, Jesus replied, is "Hear, O Israel: the Lord our God, the Lord is one; you shall love the Lord your God with all your heart, and with all your soul, and with all your mind, and with all your strength." This is a response the inquisitors could have even predicted. Jesus' reference to the opening statement of the *Shema*[16] was likely a pleasing sound to their ears. Christ answered their question, succinctly and directly. Yet his response was only beginning. He continued: "The second is this: 'You shall love your neighbor as yourself.'" As predictable as the first portion of Jesus' response was, this auxiliary dictum likely caught them unprepared.

These high-minded experts in the law were unaccustomed to such testing. Jesus' statement likening the love of people to the love of God transcended their long-held traditionalism. Their devotion to the Decalogue and the practice of their own well-established rules were legendary. Respect for another person and that person's possessions, family, and life was far from a strange notion. Yet the notion of esteeming another person on the same level as oneself made for an interesting juxtaposition with Jewish and even Roman social customs that maintained distinctions between persons of privilege and those outcast by virtue of economic, gender, health, or ethnic status.

15. Mark 12:28–34 (also Matt 22:15–22).

16. Deut 6:4–9 contains the opening portion of the *Shema*, a prayer traditionally used in Jewish worship and personal devotion; it is an affirmation of the singular holiness of the one true God. This prayer would likely have been a familiar refrain to everyone involved in this conversation.

Jesus makes yet another astounding claim—that all of the prophets and law are bound up in these two commandments.[17] The law and prophets constituted the Hebrew Scriptures, an enormous body of highly regarded and historically momentous teaching. By likening the two commandments and saying that all other prophetic and ruling principles were summed up in them, Jesus pointedly drew the inquisitors to the locus of God's reign. This is the grand liturgy of the kingdom of God: God is to be loved first and foremost with every fiber of our being and every moment of life, and treating people with dignity and care is like unto honoring God. Here Jesus laid a necessary foundation for faithfulness in worship according to the eternal kingdom of heaven.

What must become clear to the church is that faithfulness to God in worship in affect "establish[es] a world" and "worship makes available to us a different world than the one we normally inhabit."[18] As will be noted below, the church's worship in various times and places became more focused on managing life in this world with its own "settled arrangements" rather than encountering God's coming reign—present now, yet coming to its fullness. "Church," when it is faithful however, "is where we worship God by enacting and proclaiming a different set of values, a different understanding of reality."[19]

Jesus' contemporaries were confused regarding his refusal to participate in their grand schemes for gaining worldly sovereignty. That same temptation has confronted Christ's followers in every moment of the church's history. The challenge for Christ's followers is that participating in the in-breaking of this new kingdom not only seeks different meaning and ends to those of the world but also requires discernment regarding ways and means to those ends. As evidenced by Jesus Christ himself, the ways of the king-

17. Matt 22:40.
18. Lebacqz, *Word, Worship, World, & Wonder*, 64, 65.
19. Ibid., 65.

9

dom of heaven will at times conflict with the ways of the world's established practices.

Jesus came saying, in effect, by his life, teachings, and ministry, that the way the world operates—its cultures, societies, nations, and values—is irrelevant to the reign of God. Christ came to call people to participate in the irrupting reign of God, which has a vastly different tenor to it than worldly structures or entities. Much of the mystery of the kingdom of heaven is "that it is rooted in a new reality, a new social order, a new way of doing things."[20] Yet it is not enough that God's reign defines a distinct reality. The divinity-in-humanity of the Lord Jesus Christ is a signal this new reign must be lived, even if at immense risk.

LITURGY AND KINGDOMNESS

The dynamic fusion of love of God and love of people as outlined by Jesus invests liturgical exigency in the participation of God's people in the continuing in-breaking of the kingdom of heaven. It is essential to grasp the deep implications of what is perhaps one of the most misunderstood yet meaningful and necessary words to understanding worship—the word *liturgy*. The word derives its meaning from the Greek *leitourgia*, a word commonly found originally in the official idiolect of Greek city-states; it described service rendered by individuals or groups "on behalf of the political community."[21] Like the use of the term *ekklesia* (which has similar heritage), the use of such a term from the broader culture indicates the perception of the Christians that their faith community had political connotations.

Liturgy is certainly the work of the people of God in worship. Described in that phrase, liturgy exists as a functional characteristic of communal worship. It is service rendered to God by all participants through various acts and elements of worship

20. Kenneson and Street, *Selling Out the Church*, 153.
21. Wannenwetsch, *Political Worship*, 160.

in a communal setting. Yet the term has lost much of its patina within many free-church traditions. A resistance to the use of any traditional liturgy has itself become a *de facto* liturgy, with deeply entrenched patterns of various acts and elements. Even further, the exclusive use of the term in reference to corporate worship settings has limited its meaning among many faith communities, representing a formalistic approach to worship largely devoid of worth or vitality.

True liturgy, however, does not limit itself there. The liturgical dynamic has a profound effect upon the communal identity, becoming more than simple function. The whole range of actions form the community since "a group of people become something corporately which they had not been as a mere collection of individuals—*a whole greater than the sum of its parts*" (emphasis mine).[22] Deeply embedded in the Spirit-life of Christ's followers is the need to be connected to other Christ-followers. We are incomplete without one another; our common faith is collectively more than our personal devotion. The service of the body is a greater witness than the efforts of any one part by itself.

It finds fulfillment as it extends itself beyond communal gatherings to permeate every dimension of life. In its broadest sense of meaning, we are reminded that even the most simple day-in-day-out events and activities can be invested with kingdom significance. An even more profound expression is derived from the teachings of Eastern Orthodoxy, wherein this work of the people of God in worship becomes *the liturgy after the liturgy*—as work on behalf of the world. This lies at the heart of this grand liturgy of the kingdom of God: service to the world co-inheres with service to God in worship. The church is ultimately "a *leitourgia*, a ministry, a calling to act in this world after the fashion of Christ, to bear testimony to Him and His kingdom."[23]

22. Schmemann, *For the Life of the World*, 25.
23. Ibid.

There is, then, an incarnational liturgical vibrancy for followers of Christ as agents of God's kingdom in the world. Without this liturgical agency on behalf of the world, liturgical expression in communal gathering for worship is incomplete. The two do not diverge one from the other; the liturgy lived in the world for the sake of Christ is a fulfillment of the liturgical celebration of God's supreme worth and eternal redemptive activity.

PRACTICING THE REIGN

The fullness of the concept of liturgy must be reclaimed for the sake of wholeness of the gospel. If allowed to regain its fullness, this term can create space within which Christ's followers can encounter, respond to, and participate in Christ's claims upon all realms of life and creation. Liturgy can encompass a wide range of practices in which Christ's followers participate. From its earliest days to the present, the church has nurtured a rich heritage of various practices intended to enliven the faith.

Practices can be taken to mean "things Christian people do together over time to address fundamental human needs in response to and in the light of God's active presence for the life of the world in Jesus Christ."[24] A partial catalog of such things includes prayer, reading Scripture, silence and mediation, confession, singing and making music, and fasting. Also, the keeping of Sabbath, a simple water bath to signal repentance, and deliverance remembered around bread and cup are biblically robust practices that lay at the heart of the faith. In the manner of Jesus' prophetic practice, bringing good news to the poor and announcing release to captives and revealing sight to the blind and freeing those who are oppressed sum up the proclamation of God's lavish kingdom grace.[25]

---

24. Dykstra and Bass, "A Theological Understanding," 18.
25. Luke 4:16–19; Isa 61:1–2.

Why not list worship in the above litany of practices? Simply this: while worship may appear in many sources as a single practice among others, it would be more accurate for God's people to understand worship as the sum total of all practices engaged in faithfully. For the purposes of this book, faithful worship among Christ's followers is defined as *an ongoing and recurring response to the person and work of the triune God, expressed as a discipline of coming to agreement with God about who and what is holy and true and right, with the result being the church enacting and embodying the gospel of God's kingdom for the glory of God and for the sake of the world.*[26]

For Christians, then, practicing the reign of God is living in the reality of the kingdom of God—expressed in Jesus Christ, empowered by Holy Spirit—present now *in* but *not of* the world, in full anticipation of fullness of God's kingdom to come. Worship faithful to this practice of God's reign is by necessity specific, exclusive, Christologic, cosmic, and eschatological.[27]

This worship is specific because it is focused on the one true holy triune God identified in God's Word in the story of ancient Israel and revealed in Jesus Christ as the Word enfleshed. It is exclusive because it gives no quarter to any other gods regardless of their claims of god-hood; idolatry is unequivocally repudiated. It is Christologic because there is no encounter with God apart from Christ; all that is necessary for worship and life comes through him and him alone. It is cosmic because it acknowledges God's magnificent sovereignty over all creation, to be made whole under the fullness of God's reign in Christ upon the appearance of the new heaven and new earth.[28] It is eschatological because by participating in the reality of God's kingdom in the present moment in Christ, the church tells the world the story of its ultimate trans-

---

26. This definition appeared in a shorter version earlier in Hewell, "Faithful Worship," 345.

27. Ibid., 345–349.

28. Rev 21:1.

formation when the return of Christ signals the end of human-formed history and the commencement of the fullness of God's glorious eternal reign in Christ.

These kingdom-focused worship practices are interwoven into the pages that follow. The purpose is to clearly sound the urgency of the demanding yet necessary endeavor of faithfulness in all things—and in particular to the church's witness through its allegiance, affections, and actions.

2

Worship Against the World
for the Sake of the World[1]

THE FIRST followers of Christ learned to live out their faith in an imperial age when assigning the title of lord to anyone other than Caesar was to commit a radical act of sedition. To concur with Jesus' claim that God's reign was preeminently and ultimately sovereign over all creation was to deny that role to any other entity. Rome, and more specifically Caesar, was accustomed to a transcendent place in its world; to assign ultimacy to any other was to diminish Caesar and to relegate the authority of Roman rule to lower standing. Yet these Christians used precisely that language in declaring their fidelity: Jesus Christ is Lord.

Challenges to Rome's hegemonic impulse and Caesar's rule were nothing new. The Romans took on all challengers, always confident of their ability to exert their will. All claims against them were summarily rebuked with force, generally with great success and even greater fanfare. Any victorious refutation of a calculating challenger or a rising rebellion made for useful propaganda across the imperial domain. Rome's story was legend, its power mythical, and its heroes divine. Force was also used against these who followed this new king Jesus the Christ, and within a few decades the hints of decline for Rome's rule would become evident.

Jesus' life, ministry, and teachings offered a vastly different view of the beginning, course, and ending of history. Christ's proc-

1. The wording of this chapter title is borrowed with acknowledgement to Berger and Neuhaus, *Against the World for the World*.

lamation of God's coming reign over all creation ultimately would demand acknowledgement from Rome and its supposedly divine Caesar. The post-resurrection, post-ascension followers who aligned themselves with a new community, born in the sweeping Spirit-event of Pentecost, were bound together under a new allegiance to an eternal Sovereign.

From the outset, these new followers of Christ found themselves at odds with the prevailing culture of their day. Their understanding of the source, meaning, and end of life was radically different. Their identity evolved within a larger, even diverse, society. Yet they were not capriciously radical, at least not in the way revolutionaries historically assail the establishment. This new Way was radical to the core of all things, energized by a conception of reality distinct from Rome's. "[R]adicalism arises because [of an] understanding of the very meaning of the world [that] differs, often sharply, from the understanding of the dominant culture."[2] The Way of Jesus Christ was a rival for the prize of determining the ultimacy of meaning to all things, not for control of the empire. Revolutionaries tend to covet the opportunity to reinvent the reality within which they live. These new Christians were living a radical new reality, not merely a reinvention of the existing one.

Standing ahead of Christ's followers in the matter of resistance to imperial claims of ultimacy was a long heritage of Jewish culture and history. This was the story of Israel, whose covenant heritage with the Creator-God called for the formation of a nation. An element of the character of this covenant was that Israel was to be distinct from all the other nations on the face of the earth. That the journey of this nation, which was to be light to all other nations, had taken a divergent path from its original establishment did not diminish the high calling to a distinct way of being in the world. In the narrative of the first testament the Jewish nation was to be forever allied intensely with the LORD God, in whom its liturgical and political identities were inextricably bound.

2. Carter, *God's Name in Vain*, 26.

Jesus' radical claims about a new kingdom were prefigured by a long-standing anticipation that God would send a Messiah to restore the vibrancy of the Israelite nation. Jesus' life and ministry on earth developed in a hotbed of zealotry. Resistance to Roman rule was evident, as was opposition to co-oppression by elite Jewish citizens and even the temple leaders who lorded it over the common folk of Judea and Galilee.[3] Resistance to worldly sovereigns of any sort—Roman or otherwise—was not easy, nor was it always deemed appropriate. Yet resistance found a source of encouragement in Israelite understanding that God and God alone was king, a concept well delineated in the Mosaic covenant and the historic governance of these people.

For Israelites who attempted to honor the Law faithfully, worshiping this God properly meant refusing deific standing to any other god or gods. In like manner, for these new people of God in the first century, attention to God in Christ challenged their allegiance to all worldly entities and persons. "Properly understood, worship of God, and of Jesus as the unique divine Son of the one God, also involve[d] withholding of worship and unqualified obedience from any other who may claim it."[4]

The temptation to serve other gods adored by other nations haunted Israel from its earliest beginnings. The nation's collective infidelity was idolatry with political as well as religious implications. This was "a nation seeking security from . . . pagan god[s], rather than from Yahweh."[5] In one sentinel example of the nation's tendency to refute its true identity, the elders of Israel asked Samuel, "Give us a king to govern us."[6] The LORD clarified to Samuel that the people were rejecting the LORD as their sovereign. The people were unconvinced by God's cautionary explanation about the likely consequences of such an arrangement. The people were

3. Horsley, *Jesus and Empire*, 86.

4. Hurtado, *At the Origins of Christian Worship*, 116.

5. Webber and Clapp, *People of the Truth*, xx.

6. 1 Sam 8:6b.

adamant in their refusal to hear Samuel saying "'No!' but we are determined to have a king over us, so that *we also may be like all the other nations* . . .'" (emphasis mine).[7] Ancient Israel's desire to "be like all the other nations" led to a catastrophic period in their history. Their idolatry in this instance was not that they chose to be political rather than non-political. It was, rather, that they chose to trade the politics of their national identity as the people of God for the political modes of nations that did not follow the God of Abraham, Isaac, and Jacob.

The Judeans and Galileans among whom Jesus lived were acquainted with an established, if not always successful, tradition of anti-imperial patterns of action. Yet Christ's followers would come to a completely different comprehension of the ways and means of life. That comprehension exhibited itself in their manner of living, speaking, and relating to all persons and entities around them. They accepted their new minority status willingly, stepping to the margins of the prevailing society in order to follow Jesus. Ironically, they became a force that required response. Their quiet refusal to affirm the religious status quo served notice of their fidelity to this new communal identity. These Christ-followers took exception to Rome's imperial narrative of the past, present, and the future of the world. They chose to follow Christ in a radical engagement of the world as defined by the Roman establishment, the culture it engendered, and of formalistic Judaism itself.

The centerpiece of world domination prior to, during, and for three centuries following the life of Jesus Christ was the Roman Empire. At the Empire's core was the imperial cult—for all intents and purposes what might be called a state church—which represented the sum total of Rome's values and essence bound up in the identity of Caesar. The cult's stories, celebrations, and symbols combined to create a sacrosanct myth designed to reinforce Roman rule. To the extent that rule could be kept by captivating the imaginations—and thus the lives and loyalties—of the people, Roman

7. 1 Sam 8:19b–20a.

18

rule could be relatively peaceful and benevolent. To the extent that peoples' imaginations—and thus their lives and loyalties—were resistant to the myth, Roman rule was willing and capable of being coercive and cruel, in deadly measure if necessary.

Caesar's identity was highly venerated in as much as the imperial cult had religious as well as political dimensions. Messianic language was not uncommon in honoring even Caesar since he was acknowledged as the source of security and peace. It was not uncommon for Caesar to be called savior and lord.[8] The act of proclaiming that anyone other than Caesar was lord was, therefore, not just an act of treason. It was also a statement of religious disloyalty. To acknowledge there was another king, one named Jesus, was beyond doubt a daring act.

Any attempt to understand Jesus apart from this political milieu results in an abridged notion of the fullness of Jesus' life, teachings, and ministry. It is necessary to understand that "early Christian reverence of Christ was at the same time a religious act and also one with profound political connotations and consequences."[9] The political climate of Jesus' day, as well as that of his followers in the early years of the *ekklesia*, provides us a proper context for hearing the teachings of Jesus with their political connotation intact. Yet these political associations do not trade on the power of worldly entities, but find their influence revealed within the sovereignty of God guided by God's Spirit.

The genesis of *ekklesia* was predicated upon Christ's commissioning statement and the promise of the coming of Holy Spirit not long following his ascension.[10] Certainly the incarnation of God in Christ and the remarkable arrival of Holy Spirit at Pentecost constituted a singularly unified theophany. Yet the necessity of God's presence was a persistent reality in the story of ancient Israel. Moses recognized the significance of God's pres-

8. Horsley, *Religion and Empire*, 99.
9. Hurtado, *At the Origins of Christian Worship*, 117.
10. Acts 1.

ence while interceding on behalf of Israel following the nation's idolatry of the golden calf. Regarding the utter necessity of God's presence, Moses said, "In this way, we shall be distinct, I and your people, from every people on the face of the earth."[11] In this moment, Moses identifies a prime characteristic of God's people: they will be unique among all peoples, and God's presence is essential to that uniqueness.

The narrative of the establishment of the church gives abundant evidence of the effects of God's presence through Holy Spirit.[12] The startling manifestation of the Spirit in, among, and through Christ's followers huddled together following his ascension resulted in a bold multi-lingual proclamation of the gospel resulting in numerous conversions. Peter's sermon began with Joel's prophecy regarding the pouring out of God's Spirit and culminated in serving notice to the Jews that God had make Jesus Christ to be both Lord and Messiah, the very Jesus they crucified. With more than three thousand new converts, they began a distinct communal journey characterized by gracious unity, attention to the apostle's teaching, provision for the needs of all, and the praise of God. They were held in good esteem by other people, and their numbers increased.

One of the key lessons of Acts is that God's Holy Spirit will not make Christ's followers more like the world—only more and more capable of enacting and embodying the gospel as a sign to the world that the kingdom of God has come near. At every turn, the proclamation of the message regarding Jesus Christ stood in stark contrast to the values of the culture within which Christ's followers lived. In many of these instances, as well as throughout the early centuries of the expansion of the church, the gospel was increasingly repelled if not rejected, and Christ's followers were persecuted and even martyred. Regardless of such forceful dismissal of the message and messengers of Christ, the gospel spread

11. Exod 33:16b.
12. Acts 2.

throughout the whole of the Roman imperium, and ultimately beyond.

In one instance Paul and Silas arrived in Thessalonica.[13] Paul preached Jesus as Messiah on three Sabbaths, proclaiming to all in attendance that it had been necessary for Jesus to suffer and die. While some of these Jews joined Silas and Paul in following the Christ, others gathered some ruffians to stir up the crowd against them. Unable to locate the two itinerate preachers, they went to the house of Jason—a person of faith, we assume, who had been hospitable to Paul and Silas—and took him before the city authorities. The crowd was shouting that Paul and Silas were among those whose message about the Christ was turning the world upside down. The concept of turning the world upside down was a common accusation of anyone acting in a seditious manner against Roman rule. They were threatening the status quo, and the local citizens were anything but pleased. Even more so, the charges this crowd brought against Paul and Silas were political in character: "They are all acting contrary to the decrees of the emperor, saying there is another king named Jesus." It would appear even those who stood against these Christians were well aware of the political implications of the teachings of this Jesus and the words and actions of his followers.

Rome and its Caesar had seen many challengers come and go, yet the issue here is not just that Jesus was being proclaimed as a competing sovereign. "In confessing Jesus as '*the* Lord' and '*the* Son of God', these early Christians unavoidably, and often quite knowingly, denied this sort of status to the Roman ruler."[14] God was present fully in Jesus Christ to proclaim the eventual replacement of all worldly rulers and regimes. Jesus' assertions, echoed by his followers, challenged Caesar's imperial as well as divine status. In so doing, they also disputed the foundation and authority of all worldly kingdoms. In light of Jesus' claims, Caesar was

13. Acts 17:1–9.
14. Hurtado, *At the Origins of Christian Worship*, 117.

forced to promote himself as a messiah in order to save the world as he knew it; prosperity and safety—his own as well as that of the Empire—were at stake. Salvation for the realm had come from Caesar. On the other hand, Jesus declared salvation was at hand in the initiation of the kingdom of God.

One need only look at the nature of Jesus' death from the imperial perspective to gain an appreciation for the political repercussions of his life, teachings, and ministry. Roman rulers were quick to dispose of any movements or claimants to rule even faintly posing a threat to the imperial order. The placard on Jesus' cross attested to the threat he posed to the prevailing powers. The notice proclaiming that he was "the king of the Jews" was more than sarcasm. The Roman Empire was silencing another contender to its sovereignty and to its Caesar's divinity (even if they did so with the complicity of Jewish religious leaders).

Whether Jewish or Gentile by physical birth, these participants in the first *ekklesia* cast a silhouette of a story of radical citizenship across the world's stage, one differing vastly from the prevailing worldview. *Ekklesia* was a rather common term, used to denote a gathering of citizens in a Greek city-state for the purposes of making both political and judicial decisions. They chose this political nomenclature to describe their unified identity. Christ had called them from the world, and their choice of this word "made a radical declaration about their relationship to God and to the world."[15] They came to understand they had a new citizenship.[16] One can scarcely make any claim regarding citizenship without being political. To ignore the explicit use of political imagery[17] by these first

15. Bartley, *Subversive Manifesto*, 142.

16. C.f. Eph 2:19 and Phil 3:20.

17. Webber and Clapp suggest that the terminology used to describe Jesus and the mission on which he came was political. "'Kingdom' itself was a term borrowed from politics. 'Gospel' was used within the cult of the Roman emperor to refer to the announcement of the birth of an heir to a throne, an heir's coming of age, or his accession to the throne. Even 'Christ' was a title with political weight, referencing a person who was designated as a ruler."

followers of Christ is to diminish the emerging influence of their embryonic community. Disregarding such imagery weakens the gospel as well. While further commentary on the politicality of Jesus follows below, suffice it to say at this point that a depoliticized Jesus is a deficient Jesus.

These first followers of Christ carried about in their living the very radicality to which God had called them. Yet since the early days of the *ekklesia*, a variety of influences throughout the centuries has systematically truncated that radicality. One result is the church has been all too willing to accept a redefined ecclesiology, denying its prophetic and apostolic roots in favor of a more culturally accommodating posture. Another result is the church's worship has become shrouded by interwoven agendas only dimly consistent with the gospel.

Deep into the evening preceding Christ's arrest, trial, crucifixion, and death, Jesus prayed to his Father that those who would follow him would be able to be *in* the world, but *not of* the world.[18] Every word of Jesus is charged with the force of eternity, and this is no mere thought spoken lightly. Within this concept, which is anything but a finely nuanced distinction, lies an allusion to the nature of the gospel. It also defines the character of those who worship God incarnate in Christ. It demarcates the church's dynamic and creative engagement with the world. The church's most daring and effectual engagement will occur through a proper interpretation of what it means to be *in* but *not of* the world. The question is not *if* the followers of Christ will engage the world; it is, rather: What will be the *nature* of that engagement?

In one sense, the gospel tells us of God in Christ taking a radical stand *against* the world. Again, "Jesus Christ is the supreme divine intrusion into the world's settled arrangements."[19] These "settled arrangements" are the world's ways of operating

Webber and Clapp, *People of the Truth*. 40.

18. Taken primarily from John 17:13–19.

19. Hauerwas and Willimon, *Resident Aliens*, 51.

and organizing itself which, at best, are only dimly consistent with truth. Christ's stories, miracles, and conversations with people were provocative challenges to the prevailing ways of the world. His death on the cross is evidence enough that his challenges did not go unnoted. His resurrection gave birth to a tidal-wave movement which merely reinforces the impact of the intrusive nature of Christ's gospel. In this sense, the gospel is radical; it challenges the world and the world's ways of being at every point.

Yet it is part of the paradox of the gospel that God in Christ also takes a radical stand *on behalf of* the world. Christ is an advocate before God for the world. God came in Christ to make the good news of God's reign clear if not comprehensible. The reconciling work of Christ changes everything and offers redemption and restoration to all of creation.[20]

Understanding the gospel requires acknowledging the dual impulses of "in but not of." The gospel makes radical claims on our lives, and we become followers of Jesus. And like Jesus, Christ's followers make choices against the world as well as acting on behalf of the world, living the gospel—the good news—into the world. The church exists for the glory of God and for the sake of the world, a dialectic balance requiring the church to be in the world without being of the world.

These dynamically corresponding impulses—in but not of the world—have been identified as "The Twin Forces of Christian History."'[21] These two forces both find their source within the gospel itself, and must be held in continuous tension. The first is the "*indigenizing principle* . . . a homing instinct, which creates in diverse communities a sense that the church belongs there" (emphasis mine).[22] The second is the "*pilgrim principle* that creates within the Christian community the sense that it is not fully at home in this world, *so that it comes into tension with its society from its loyalty*

20. 2 Cor 5:18–19.
21. Walls, *The Missionary Movement in Christian History*, 53.
22. Ibid.

24

to Christ" (emphasis mine).[23] The jeopardy in the first without sufficient measure of the second allows the church and its gospel to become too much "at home" in the culture within which it exists. The hazard of the second without sufficient measure of the first is that the church might isolate itself and its gospel from the culture within which it exists. In either case the church's witness and the gospel's influence are diminished, one because of a lack of distinction from the culture, the other because it is too far removed for viable persuasion. The greater danger is not to have too much of either impulse—only to have too little of one or the other.

Faithful worship and the church's liturgy, defined as the work of the people of God, will intensify rather than abate the dynamic tension of *in* but *not of*. Such worship will shape participants for living both the indigenizing and pilgrim principles of the gospel. The gospel expressed faithfully through the lives of Christ's followers will always challenge the world's "settled arrangements" and serve the world for the world's sake.

Any examination of the biblical record reveals the radical nature of all encounters with the God of Israel incarnate in Christ. Descriptions of encounters with God throughout history reveal the LORD God to be graciously confrontational. If followers of Christ respond faithfully to these radical encounters, the world will perceive the church—and its subsequent engagement with the world—as radical. As bearers of the message of Christ his followers are likely to threaten the status quo, turning the world upside down as it were, as per the assessment of the citizens of Thessalonica after Silas and Paul came to town. The church's presentation of an alternative way of being in the world will challenge the world's ways of being, its "settled arrangements."

God was in Christ, not reconciling Godself to the world, but reconciling the world to Godself.[24] The standard for evaluation is not the world; the standard for evaluation is God. The church faces

23. Ibid., 54.
24. 2 Cor 5:18–19.

a great temptation in attempting to be like the world in order to reach the world. Without caution, the measure of the church's consonance with the ways of the world can also become the measure of the church's dissonance with the reign of God. The attraction is participation in a form of atheistic practicality,[25] described as thinking the church can best communicate the gospel by being like the world. To wit: "The church's great temptation is to make the good news easy by adapting it to systems and ideologies that are already congenial and demand little sacrifice, and make little difference in the world."[26] God demands that God's people live in ways which are distinct from the world. The notion that this demand does not matter will always produce idolatry.

The church's ability to live out the gospel on behalf of the world is predicated upon its ability to make and keep commitments that cause the church to be distinct from the world. Put the other way round, only by making choices against what the world stands for can the church be in any position at all to act liturgically for the world's benefit. The church exists for the glory of God and for the sake of the world; only by being faithful in the former will the church ever do anything that matters in regard to the latter.

The world will not understand those who choose to follow Christ; he was clear on this point. Yet if Christ's followers are faithful, they become salt and light, causing the world to discover in them a "warrant for belief."[27] The world's only hope is for Christ's followers to accept a measure of a perceived dissonance with the world's self-perceptions for the sake of helping the world see itself clearly in contrast to God's kingdom in Christ. If the world too readily recognizes itself in the church, the world will not see itself for what it really is. The world will welcome a distorted view of

25. Such an atheism "is the conviction that the presence and power of God are unessential to the work of ministry, that we can find the right technique, the proper approach, and the appropriate attitude and therefore will not need God to validate our ministry" Willimon, *The Intrusive Word*, 22.

26. Webber and Clapp, *People of the Truth*, 35.

27. Dawn, *A Royal "Waste" of Time*, 119.

itself propped up by a too-relevant church that affirms, accepts, and validates the world's ways of being.

The tension of *in* but *not of*, an essential yet temporal part of the reality of God's kingdom born in Christ, creates the gospel's opportunity to speak to the world's deepest needs. "[The Christian community] exists . . . to set up in the world a new sign that is radically dissimilar to [the world's] own manner and which *contradicts it in a way which is full of promise*" (emphasis mine).[28] The church lives in contradistinction to the world, in order to communicate the full promise of the gospel to the world.

It is not enough for the church to merely offer a critique of the world. The church exists as what can be called a "diacritical community."[29] To be a critic is to do nothing more than identify the failings of the other. But "the diacritic goes one step further and distinguishes an alternative . . . [presenting] a distinctive, alternative identity and vision."[30] The church exists to tell the world the story of its future; it is "the social configuration that concretely signifies to the world its destiny in the age to come."[31] Only as the church offers the promise of God's reign for all of creation does it fulfill its role as steward of God's eternal kingdom.

Faithful worship "will eventually be *subversive of the culture surrounding it*" (emphasis mine). [32] This is precisely the perspective of the public leaders of Thessalonica as they encountered the preaching of Silas and Paul: "These people who have been turning the world upside down have come here also . . ."[33] In spite of the world's perception to the contrary, the reign of God in Christ does not turn the world upside down—it will turn the world right side up. Faithful worship will nurture Christ's followers in God's truth,

28. Barth, *Church Dogmatics*, 779.

29. Webber and Clapp, *People of the Truth*, 56.

30. Ibid.

31. Harvey, *Another City*, 70.

32. Dawn, *Reaching Out Without Dumbing Down*, 57.

33. Acts 17:6b.

and only as they worship the Father in spirit and in truth will they be able to live right side up. Christ came to call people to participate in the irrupting reign of God—an in-breaking of eternal wonder and consequence. God's kingdom has a vastly different tenor to it than worldly structures or entities. The new right-side-up kingdom must be lived contemporaneously, even if at immense risk.

Implementing this new reign requires different ways and means than those of worldly powers. "Too often, it seems, the church has been tempted to believe that this new kingdom God is bringing could be established by using the methods of the old kingdom which is passing away. But part of what makes this new kingdom new is that it is rooted in a new reality, a new social order, a new way of doing things."[34] Jesus came saying, in effect, by his life, teachings, and ministry, that the way the world operates—its cultures, societies, nations, and values—is irrelevant to the reign of God.

FAITHFUL WORSHIP

The irrupting reign of God in Christ does not seek the world's approval, nor does it merely accommodate itself to the world's ways. "Worshiping communities are relevant *not* to the degree that they ask what is pleasing, attractive, or palatable to the prevailing culture. They *are* relevant if they become expert at speaking and teaching their language in different contexts."[35] The church's language is the language of faithfulness to God in Christ, and it is important for the church to learn to translate faithfulness to God into the languages of different contexts and cultures. Only then can those within the context or culture learn from the church to speak this living language of the kingdom of God's rule.

Those who follow Christ learn this language through faithful worship. The language of faithful Christian worship, as well as the

34. Kenneson and Street, *Selling Out the Church*, 153.
35. Ibid.

actions and symbols of worship, should be the language, actions, and symbols of those reconciled to God, those who have begun living in the reality of God's reign.[36] Ultimately, the language of the gospel is the language of reconciliation, bringing the world to account in regard to God's reign in Christ.

Faithful worship does not necessarily make itself accessible to those who are outside the faith. The confessions essential to faithful worship are as likely to deter some persons from participation as they are to draw others. Faithful worship forms people who are capable of understanding and apprehending the meaning of the reign of God in Christ, who can then begin to live in the new reality represented by that reign. Standing at the heart of the gospel is a call to worship the one, true, holy God. In Christ, this call is not just to the faithful, but graciously to those outside the faith as well. Thus, the church's radical encounter with the world begins with a radical encounter with God in worship.

Paul wrote to the church in Corinth regarding Christ's crucifixion as not only a stumbling block, but foolishness—the former to Jews, the latter to Gentiles.[37] If Christ's crucifixion is such to those not yet called into faith, so too will the worship of the resurrected and ascended Christ by his followers appear to the same audience.

Faithful worship will shape participants in ways that cause the world to question the validity of its own existence outside of allegiance to the one, true, sovereign God. The true worship of the LORD God by God's people will be more than a reflection of the culture within which any given congregation finds itself. Such worship will be, rather, "an embodied question mark"[38] that chal-

---

36. "Church is where we worship God by enacting and proclaiming a different set of values, a different understanding of reality." Lebacqz, *Word, Worship, World, & Wonder*, 65.

37. 1 Cor 1:20–25.

38. Poulton, *People Under Pressure*, 112.

lenges the surrounding settled arrangements, and poses this deci-sive question: What will you do with Jesus?

The radical demands of the gospel are central to the catalytic presence of the church. The church's worship should be character-ized by encounters with God which, in some measure, defy logic and comprehension by the culture within which it exists. The or-dered gathering of the faith community may well be a conundrum for the world, requiring a miracle of God's Spirit for non-believing observers to hear, see, and understand.[39] Faithful worship may re-quire Christ's followers to exhibit courage and grace, since persons outside the faith may misapprehend it. Yet the uncomprehending space created by this lack of understanding may prove valuable for faithful witness.

The first Christians—*the Christ people*—gathered regularly, and the simple liturgy they adopted centered on prayer, attention to teachings of the apostles, water, bread, the cup, and the sharing of all things for the benefit of everyone. These liturgical practices shaped and sustained their identity as resident aliens, citizens of a new order who yet resided within the old. Their very manner of being was unique; it became a living critique of the world as they knew it. Rome guarded its existence jealously. However, dis-ruption and destruction were not on the collective mind of the new community. Those were neither the mode nor goal of the first Christ-followers. Their seminal concern was their newfound al-legiance to the newly proclaimed reign of God, practiced through the habits of *ekklesia*.

All worship communicates a story, presumably freighted with temporal and eternal significance. The question is: Which story does Christian worship tell? The church's worship may be ac-curate or inaccurate as to the story of God in Scripture. "What we need in worship is the Truth—the truth, the whole truth, nothing but the truth."[40] For followers of Christ—formed as Christ's body,

39. Willimon, *The Intrusive Word*, 18, 19, 22.
40. Dawn, *A Royal "Waste" of Time*, 66.

the church—the ultimate question regarding worship is whether it will be faithful to truth as expressed into the world by God through Christ. Does worship tell the world's story, or the story of the cosmically redemptive triune God? Even more pointedly, does the church's worship enact God's story *accurately*, or does it hold hidden or not-so-hidden agendas of worldly hope?

Faithful Christian worship will always draw very precise distinctions. "The initial objective of every worship act is to make clear which God, among all the offers and claims of deity in our religiously drenched society, we are giving allegiance and obedience"[41] Any ambiguity about who or what is being worshiped will produce a proportional ambiguity in the meaning of worship. Clearly then, "The real meaning of worship derives in the first place from the God to whom it is directed."[42] The particularity of faithful worship by Christians specifies God encountered in the story of ancient Israel and in the person of Jesus Christ. It is this particular God, who speaks a particular word to us in Jesus, requiring a particular response, calling us to live in particular ways. Glory and honor are due to this particular God who alone is the one, true, holy God. This particular God asks ultimate questions, to which God ultimately expects a particular response. It is in this *particularity* that God, and our response to God, find their compelling authority. This particularity and the clarity it produces define the radical claims of the gospel and true worship of the triune God.

The clarity with which worship is vested is a vital measure of faithfulness in serving this God. Once we have come to clarity about God, we are in a position to acknowledge and come to grips with the demands God places on our lives. We are prepared to become faithful followers of Christ.

In faithful worship, Christians are habituated into the fullness of the story of ancient Israel and the person of Jesus Christ. The Creator God called Israel to be a nation, to be the only one

41. Meeks, *God the Economist*, 71–72.
42. Rowley, *Worship in Ancient Israel*, 251.

of its kind among all the peoples of the earth. "When God called Israel and claimed the people for his own, he called them into a liberating struggle against the tyranny and oppression of the political authorities in Egypt, and his goal was the establishment of Israel as his 'people,' as a political body, a nation."[43] For centuries, God's story involved God's relationship with Israel, sometimes contending on behalf of the chosen people, at other times contending with those same people. Yet the record of ancient Israel is not the fullness of God's story. "In Jesus the biblical story reaches its climax"[44] and God offers a new covenant, one extended to all persons—Gentiles as well as Jews. It is a radical act to worship the triune God revealed in the story of ancient Israel and in the person of Jesus Christ.

As the body of Christ, the church has a distinct role in God's story. "The church is the bearer to all the nations of a gospel that announces the kingdom, the reign, and the sovereignty of God."[45] The reign of God is a radical and in-breaking force in the history of all things, understood to be present, but not yet fully so. It is comprehensive in its influence, encompassing all the world's settled arrangements. The world does not fully understand God's reign and in like manner it does not understand faithful Christian worship. God's reign in Christ irrupts in response to long pent up energy in the history of creation, and will fundamentally change the nature of all life within it.

Where, then, are the followers of Jesus Christ whose communal worship causes them to live in witness to the irrupting reign of God? Where is the church whose worship makes a confident, radical, even subversive sound which trumpets the incomparable truth of God's reign, rather than tribute to any of the world's Caesars? In its superlative form, communal worship among Christ-followers is a profound affair—theologically exigent, liturgically engaging, and

43. Osborn, *The Barmen Declaration*, 99.
44. Ibid.
45. Newbigin, *Foolishness to the Greeks*, 124.

politically dynamic. It is theological in that it is centered upon the triune God. It is liturgical in that it employs God's people in active participation in a dynamic, symbolic, living language. It is political in that it shapes the faith community, which, thus formed, lives liturgically on behalf of the world. Faithful Christian worship, at its core, attends to this story and the establishment of a new order in Christ. It is one thing for this story to be treated as simply that—a story. It is quite another for it to be believed for what it is—a declaration of a new day which will come for the whole creation.

To be certain, Christians encounter God in worship *in* the world; it is appropriate since God is at work in the world, and an incarnational expression of the gospel requires Christ's followers to participate with God in God's redemptive, re-creating deeds. Yet because faithfulness in the worship of the triune God calls worshipers to a distinct way of being which contradicts the world's ways of being, it is in that sense *against* the world. The only way the world will ever benefit from such worship will be if the church honors this dynamic tension. A faithful expression of the gospel requires it to be so.

3

Nationalism Part 1:
The Allure of Triumphalism

SUPPOSE FOR the moment that the commitments and relationships inherent among God's people lack any political character whatsoever. Entertain the notion that the kinds of choices people make in joining others who have come to faith are limited to spiritual implications with some social ramifications. Consider the possibility that being a follower of Christ means having a hope for the future with little or no responsibilities for the present. Give consideration to the chance there could be realms of human life in this world standing outside the reach of God's authority and thus are of no consequence to the church and the God the church serves. What if the church as the presence of Christ in the world did not have a political bone in its body?

If the scenario highlighted in the paragraph immediately above were true, it could then be argued that the church need not concern itself with political matters. Enticement to participate in such activities could simply be resisted. Entanglements born of the intertwining of religious piety and political influence could be diminished if not totally avoided. Getting on with life in the world could just be a good bit simpler and maybe even more enjoyable. The church could just say "No" and be on its joyful merry way, if only that was all true.

The reality of the kingdom of God, however, heralds a distinctly different scenario. The reign of God in Christ, present in the world yet not of the world, requires Christians to deal with a number of ambiguities even in the face of things believed to be certain and truthful. One of the prime dilemmas is how to faithfully live out the politics of the kingdom of heaven—already present, yet awaiting its completion to come—in the midst of a world full of masters of political intuitions, intrigues, and institutionalisms born of the spirits of many ages and myths.

Throughout its history ancient Israel struggled to live up to its own political identity. The nation was formed out of a unique heritage, a dramatic exodus and journey to a gifted homeland, and a distinctive law bound together in ritual worship of holy God and ethical behavior. Their troubled history reveals a rather spotted record of encounters with a long list of nations. That record includes their own enticements to the powers of worldly nationalism, representing attempts at syncretistic appropriation of those powers.

Jesus Christ lived in a season of Israel's struggle under the hand of the Roman Empire. It was certainly not their first encounter with imperial authority; their encounters with Babylon and Assyria still held a prominent place in their collective historical memory. Within the Jewish society of Jesus' day the Sadducees compromised and participated with Roman rule, and the Herodians sought the restoration of theocracy through that same authority. The Zealots plotted revolt while the Essenes withdrew completely. Jesus' annunciation of the kingdom of his Father stood as much in contradistinction to the culture of his own people as it did to the Roman imperium. The incarnation of God in Jesus is a reminder that the gospel will always come upon worldly political entities, many of which can by rights be known as empires and many of which may have faint resonance with the truth of God's Word.

The nature of the church's message has always proven tempting. After all, resurrection is an appealing proposition. The idea that definitive peril and death could be defeated is bound to draw attention, especially when a long-prophesied Messiah is both the proclaimer and enactor of the meaning of resurrection. Salvation themes are not limited to the biblical record; they appear within all of the world's narratives, including those of societies Christians call "pagan." In a world where pain and oppression are endemic, a conquering king and a blissful kingdom always make for a good story.

Part of the life-blood of any empire is its stories. Its own national identity is bound up in narratives about its founding, struggles, victories, and values. Such tales are always nationalistic in intent; they are always biased and rightfully so. Nationalism offers little or nothing of value if it repudiates its own nation. In service to this endeavor, nationalism will seek support through any adjunct means to bolster the impact of the narrative. In general, the more grand and glorious the narrative the more stable the empire. While the more unpleasant modes of imperial history may be acknowledged, nationalism tends to prefer the voice of triumph to the cries of tragedy.

Indeed, the gospel sounds a triumphant note. To deny this would be to refute an essential element of God's grand metanarrative. However, the triumph of God's redemptive activity in history through Christ must be distinguished from its syncretistic alter ego—triumphalism. For purposes here, triumphalism is viewed as the church's syncretic patterns of thought and behavior that signal an inordinate confidence in worldly methods as the means for accomplishing the purposes of the gospel. Granted, the incarnational character of the gospel requires appropriate enculturation. The church acts triumphalistically, however, when its worship does more to form worshipers for their citizenship here in the world than it does to form them for their citizenship in the kingdom of God. Stated otherwise being *in* the world takes precedence over being *not of* the world.

Triumphalism may promote a perfunctory theology, one "in which there are no loose ends" and "is not true to life nor can it adequately reflect the richness of the gospel."[1] Such a triumphalism allows the church to live in the reality of the fullness of God's reign

1. Drane, *The McDonaldization of the Church*, 37.

to come while denying the reality of the brokenness, need, honesty, pain, and distress that exists in the *not-yet-ness* of that reign. The church tends to triumphalism when it claims the certainty of future means that present reality does not matter or has no meaning. Triumphalism treats the reality of now as something that must merely be endured until the fullness of God's reign comes. It may also treat the reality of the fullness to come as only a dim and distant hope and, thereby, invest far too heavily in the hope for the not-yet-ness of God's reign. Triumphalism may even unwittingly engage what Paul refers to as "the cosmic powers of this present darkness"[2] as the means through which God's reign can be implemented. It bears the marks of human ingenuity and wisdom more so than the inscription of God's Spirit, and may even join forces with worldly entities.[3]

Suffice it to say here that the intersection of empire and the gospel has always presented tantalizing prospects for both the church and the empire. The possibility that the church will be tempted to employ methods and messages that are inconsistent with the reign of God is inherent in the church's placement in the world. Also inherent in the church's placement in the world is the possibility that the world will be tempted to employ the church's

2. Eph 6:12.

3. In describing what he calls the "myth of progress" N.T. Wright provides these insights: "This utopian dream is in fact a parody of the Christian vision. The kingdom of God and the kingdoms of the world come together to produce a vision of history moving forward toward its goal, a goal that will emerge from within rather than being a new gift from elsewhere. Humans can be made perfect and are indeed evolving inexorably toward that point. The world is ours to discover, exploit, and enjoy. Instead of dependence on God's grace, we will become what we have the potential to be by education and hard work. Instead of creation and new creation, science and technology will turn the raw material of this world into the stuff of utopia. Like the mythical Prometheus, defying the gods and trying to run the world his own way, liberal modernism supposes that the world can become everything we want it to be by working a bit harder and helping forward the great march into the glorious future." Wright, *Surprised by Hope*, 82.

message—the gospel, and the church's method—offering alternatives for truth and transcendence, for the world's own purposes. Both of these possibilities certainly make for strange companions, both of which likely detract from the church's commitment to its calling in Christ. In the first instance, *missio Dei* is re-interpreted as *missio ecclesia*—something of a misnomer since the mission belongs to God and is bound up in the agenda of the kingdom of heaven. The church holds title to no mission of its own beyond participation in *missio Dei*. In the second, *missio mundus*—the mission of the world—takes center stage.

Clarity about its message is indispensable for the church's ability to resist triumphalism. The gospel is no less necessary for the church than it is for the world. The church must constantly re-learn the metanarrative of God encountered in the story of ancient Israel and the person of Jesus Christ. Faithful worship will enable that re-learning as an ongoing process. Triumphalism may create an unnatural euphoria among followers of Christ, who may "seem too happy to live, worship, and witness in ways that can appear to be denying some of the central themes we claim to believe in."[4] Triumphalism will skew how the church sees God and how the church sees itself. A church that inaccurately sees God and itself will lose its identity—*missio Dei*. That would be an immense misfortune for the church and ultimately for the world.

POLITICAL IDENTITY

The word *polis*, meaning city, is the Greek root for the word we understand as "politics" or "political." Accordingly, it may be said that "[a]nything is political which deals with how people live together in organized ways."[5] In like manner, the post-Pentecost *ekklesia* that grew up around loyalty to Christ could also be described as *polis*, "a nation, that is, a people with a common history and

---

4. Drane, *The McDonaldization of the Church*, 138.

5. Yoder, *For the Nations*, 223.

destiny, identity and mission."[6] The use of political terminology—
ekklesia—to describe the new community formed around these
practices was apt, and its use "made a radical declaration about
their relationship with God and the world."[7]

It would scarcely have crossed the minds of God's people, in
the times described in both the First and Second Testaments, to
separate political identity from any dimension of life, be it identified as religious or otherwise. The very nature of the *ekklesia* that
brought it into a radical and subversive encounter with Rome is
the same nature of "polity and politics that were thoroughly Jewish
from beginning to end."[8]

For the first followers of Christ the act of conversion was no
mere private issue; it was profuse with social as well as political
ramifications. The book of Acts is replete with illustrations of the
persecutions and public behavior of the disciples. The record indicates that they "were together, and held all things in common; they
would sell their possessions and goods and distribute the proceeds
to all, as any had need" and they met in the temple and in homes.[9]
The covenantal witness of their chosen places of meeting and economic relationships was powerful enough to gain the attention of
other citizens of the realm. The apostles accomplished "many won-
ders and signs" and "they ate their food with glad and generous
hearts, praising God and having the goodwill of all the people."[10]
These hardly seemed the activities of rabble rousers, yet that did
not prevent the Roman perception of the Way[11] as a subversive
fantasy. To make a conscious choice to join this group of people
required no small measure of conviction.

6. Baxter, "God is Not an American," 75.
7. Bartley, *Subversive Manifesto*, 142.
8. Harvey, *Another City*, 35.
9. Acts 2:44–46.
10. Acts 2:43, 46b–47.
11. Acts 9:2; 19:23; 22:4; 24:14, 22.

From the earliest moments of Christ's messianic declarations, persons who chose to follow had a growing sense that a decision to go with Jesus carried political significance. Even then, his closest disciples during his earthly life may have quite misunderstood the full implications of Christ's teachings. The early church, however, readily became aware that following Christ required a level of allegiance that placed distance between anyone who was loyal to Christ and any other claimant to the title of lord, such as Caesar. Loyalty was an issue of considerable prominence in the day of oppressive Roman rule. No quarter was given; all persons within the realm were expected under threat of coercion to bear loyalty to the Empire and its leaders in every sphere of life. The stand taken by those who became followers of the Way of Jesus was no less political than it was spiritual. Those identified with the Way were persecuted by the civil authorities as well as by Jewish religious leaders consorting with the civil authorities.

It is well worth noting here that the early *ekklesia* chose to declare, retain, and even value their status as a diasporic community—lacking a place to claim as their own and living as aliens in towns they neither designed nor constructed.[12] Roman law would have allowed Christ-followers to claim status as a *cultus privitas*, "dedicated to the pursuit of personal piety and other-worldly salvation."[13] They made a conscious decision, however, to forgo imperial sanction for their beliefs and behaviors. To consent to such sanction might have been perceived as complicity with Roman authority. They accepted the fact that loyalty to Christ demanded that they renounce Caesar's claims of absolute sovereignty, an obligation they willingly fulfilled.

They recognized the necessity of confronting the surrounding society with the gospel. They chose to do so "with a social and this-worldly alternative that incorporated elements of its host culture

12. Harvey, *Another City*, 18.
13. Ibid.

while remaining a distinct people."[14] The very resources and daily necessities of life were much the same for the followers of Christ as for those in their society who knew not Christ. Yet their manner of living was distinct. Their adaptation of indigenous political imagery—*ekklesia*—was intentional.

Christ's followers were indeed a subversive influence, since their "mission inherently involved calling into question long-standing assumptions about the way a people should order the relations between citizens with those outside their own particular community."[15] Rather than seeking imperial sanction or subsisting out of sight from Roman authority, the *ekklesia* was emboldened by its faith to live openly as a communal critique of its surrounding culture.

The presence of the faith community was intentionally provocative. *Ekklesia's* unique bond of fellowship ignored socio-economic, gender, and ethnic bias and embraced people from all tribes, nations, and languages. Its unity proved to be a "visible basis for the gospel's power and legitimacy."[16] The invitation extended in the gospel truly represented then, as it does now, a call to a new way of being in relation to God and others making it possible "to enter the reign-of-God produced community of the new humanity."[17]

No doubt these new relationships were a challenge to Christ's followers in the first century *ekklesia*. While these distinctions still hold sway in the present day, followers of Christ in the twenty-first century—like these first century disciples—have no business acting in ways that legitimize such biased separations. The trans-temporal, trans-spatial *ekklesia* that claims to follow Christ in all times and in all places bears witness to the new political order under the reign of God.

14. Ibid., 18.
15. Ibid., 19.
16. Guder, *Missional Church*, 104.
17. Ibid.

The establishment of this community as the living emblem and foretaste of the reign of God in Christ was a bold divine creative act. The powers and rulers of this world have no standing by which to define the ultimate meaning of history. That role belongs to the body of Christ—the church. It is through the church that the wisdom of God is made manifest to the rulers and authorities, even in the heavenly places.[18] To say that the community of Christ's followers known as the church is merely the deliverer of the message of the gospel or simply the offspring of the gospel is to understate its nature in God's redemptive endeavor. The *ekklesia's* primary witness to the world, in the first century as well as in our day, is *"the corporate life of the believing community"* (emphasis mine).[19] This re-created relationship to God, to other persons, and even to creation itself is the good news—enfleshed for the world to see in the church.

CONSTANTINIANISM'S LEGACY

The church's ongoing struggle for faithfulness is inherent in the reality of its existence in the world. Living in tension between the demands of the gospel and the demands of the world has never been an easy task. The mantle of the gospel had been laid by Christ on the shoulders of his body, the church. For the most part the church has worn the mantle well, although not without challenges to the rightful ownership of that mantle. Those challenges have come both from within and without the church itself. The early history of the church reveals first a struggle for survival. A hard-won stability then paved the way for increasing communication and organization among far-flung local congregations, many of which began to rely on their own unique local identity against the backdrop of a rapidly expanding human population. The seeds of institutionalism sprouted as a hierarchy of ecclesial authority

18. Eph 3:10.
19. Dawn, *How Shall We Worship?*, 45.

sought to superintend the rising influence of the church and the gospel of its Lord. Thus the stage was set for the church's encounter with a variety of other systematized influences.

A dramatic change in the relationship between the church and empire would ultimately contribute to the dissection of life into sacred and secular, religious and political, physical and spiritual, temporal and eternal. This dichotomous transition would become an impediment to the gospel. Politics and faith, once viewed as an integrated whole of life, became uneasy partners throughout much of history producing a checkered record for both. The mechanism was in place for the disablement of the political nature of God's redemptive activity in the world.

The church's primary political dilemma has centered on the enticements of nationalism (also referred to here as empire). During *ekklesia's* earliest decades, the authority of the Roman imperial realm tended more toward persecution than it did any semblance of partnership. For nearly three centuries the body of Christ lived out is communal identity on the margins of society, even as the gospel spread rapidly across the populations of the known world. This early sense of Christ-following as an alternative way of being in community continued to the early fourth century. By that time the church's fortunes had changed considerably by some accounts. Local congregations were present and visible throughout the Empire, with some villages being almost thoroughly Christian. With the increased visibility "Christians were becoming respected members of society and their ideas were increasingly influential."[20] Once it became evident that the Way was unlikely to diminish, much less disappear, the responses of imperial sovereigns turned from dismissal to tolerance and eventually to alliance.

It should come as no surprise that Constantine would develop an interest in the movement after recognizing the relative instability of his increasingly multicultural Empire. A religious movement that had the power to unite persons across ethnic, cultural,

20. Murray, *Post-Christendom*, 28.

and economic boundaries held great promise for providing unity throughout the realm. The wellbeing of the Empire could benefit from an established Christianity, which in turn could benefit from the wellbeing of sponsoring imperial power. The emperor lifted the ban on public expressions of Christianity and gatherings for worship, a decidedly political decision aimed at nothing less than an attempt to leverage the momentum of the followers of Christ on behalf of his own rule and status in the Empire. By the time Theodosius proclaimed Christianity as the official religion of the Roman Empire in 380, the Christian faith was more than publicly legal. It had, in fact, moved to the center of society.

Imperial leaders were astute politicians and opportunists who knew the value of leveraging every possible force for the benefit of their rule. They grasped "the potential of religious ideas for shaping the Empire"[21] and sought to use them to uphold the Empire's institutions and unite its citizens. The centralization of Christianity as the state religion diminished the distinction of polity between the Empire and the *ekklesia* of Christ's followers.[22]

Prior to its establishment at the locus of Roman society, the church as *ekklesia* was relatively *ad hoc*. Following its move to the hub of society, promoting the values of the dominant governing body made sense. With its newfound position came a structural shift that in many ways imitated the imperial system of jurisdictions and ranks for citizens. The church's need for larger spaces in which to gather increased as imperial inducements for conversion produced a near flood of new believers.

As a result, the church grew in size and stature within Roman society. In addition to the status and power accrued to bishops in

21. Ibid., 29.

22. It is necessary to note that church before Constantine was not necessarily always at its best. Further, the transformation of the relationship between the church and state in Constantianism and all that followed did not mean that the church became a failure. The church did, however lose something of its original sense of identity, found in *missio Dei*, an identity that must be regained in our day.

an increasingly hierarchical structure, the church also became increasingly wealthy and socially prominent due to the influx of persons of greater means and higher station in society. During its first three centuries of existence, the church had largely maintained a sense of unity that transcended ethnic, socio-economic, and gender restrictions. The church now found itself faced with the need to make adjustments for its increasingly influential converts as membership brought public benefits. The trans-partisanism of the early *ekklesia* was bowing to the partisan ways of the pagan world within which it enjoyed an increasingly more potent position.

It was a general assumption that the gospel had triumphed over the Empire, and that God had acted to vindicate the church after three centuries of marginal existence and oppression. However, rather than setting things aright per the reign of God that *ekklesia's* Messiah had come to proclaim, this distorted the church's view of itself. The result was an imperial church[23] whose identity was ultimately as closely tied to the Empire as it was to the gospel of Christ, if not more so. The shift created by Constantine's decision and the church's willing participation in the process meant that "the church decided to derive its significance through association with the identity and purposes of the state."[24]

The church's alliance with the Roman Empire produced more entanglement with the Empire's agenda than freedom to pursue *missio Dei* faithfully. It was now necessary for the Christ's followers to face the challenge that it continues to face even to this day: how to live out the gospel *in* the empire, without being *of* the empire.

Approximately one century passed from the time the Christian faith became the official religion of the Empire and the fall of Rome. The Empire's disintegration and demise, however, was fended off long enough for the partnership between church and the state to be well formed. To be sure, it was a powerful partnership as "[t]he church provided religious legitimation for state

23. Hall, *The End of Christendom and the Future of Christianity*, 1.
24. Clapp, *A Peculiar People*, 25.

activities [and] the state provided secular support for ecclesiastical decisions."[25] In the face of the Empire's hegemonic tendencies, the church's vested interest turned to the sustenance of the imperial status quo.

The demise of the Empire paved the way for the rise of medieval Christendom, which maintained its course of a religion-dominated society for much of a one thousand year period. The following is an apt description of that establishment:

> What is beyond dispute is that Christendom developed into a society that excluded or marginalised other religious options, where almost everyone regarded themselves as Christians and accepted without question a Christian worldview. The biblical story, the authority of the church and Christian terminology and concepts were imbibed through liturgy, art, sculpture, music, literature, architecture, legislation, customs and language. And people believed in Christendom itself as a Christian civilisation that provided a framework for political, economic, social, military and cultural life.[26]

Christendom can be identified succinctly as "the dominion or sovereignty of the Christian religion."[27] While it is an alluring proposition on its face, no one should confuse Christendom with the *ekklesia* of the followers of Christ, the community that practices the politics of God's reign. Over the course of its influence, Christendom would eventually make it possible to redefine faith. Christendom became "Christianity without Jesus at the centre,"[28] which effectively meant that the political implications of Christ's life, teachings, and ministry were laid aside.

Coercion became a common theme in the extension of Christendom's influence. Force was a regular implement of the social structure characterized by missionary zeal and cultural supe-

---

25. Murray, *Post-Christendom*, 84.
26. Ibid., 66.
27. Hall, *The End of Christendom and the Future of Christianity*, ix.
28. Murray, *Post-Christendom*, 311.

riority.[29] With a rise in the church's influence came an absolutism as to what people should believe and how they should live their lives. Christendom became a culture of totalitarian dimensions, dealing severely with anyone who dared create dissension or challenge its beliefs.[30] While the prime threat to the early *ekklesia* was the Roman imperium, the post-Constantinian church tended to side with the imperium to sanction and safeguard the imperium's status.

The marks of Christendom are broad and deep. Arguably, the world gained a concept of religion less like *ekklesia* and more like empire. The methodology of one became indistinguishable from that of the other. As the two entities became more closely entangled, to think of empire was to think of the church, and vice versa. Because of its response to Constantinianism-become-Christendom, the church lost the sense of itself as an alternative *polis*.[31]

Christendom ultimately was unable to sustain the ability to exercise political action that could transcend the rising nationalistic impulses of Europe and the West. The rise of the modern nation-state was on the horizon. The church's "caesaropapist" alliance with partisan, reactionary political power produced a reversal of significant proportions.[32] The inversion of supreme authority and the subjugation of ecclesial hierarchy to newly vested civil rulers cost the church even more than Constantinianism. "[T]he church was relieved of its separate jurisdictional authority and redefined as a purely suasive body, allowing the state to become the absolute and unquestioned political authority."[33] The church's transformation to apolitical status was well underway as the state was becoming the arena of all political activity.

29. Brown, *The Rise of Western Christendom*, 41.
30. Murray, *Post-Christendom*, 68.
31. Clapp, "Practicing the Politics of Jesus," 23.
32. Herbert, *Religion and Civil Society*, 25.
33. Harvey, *Another City*, 80.

Two other significant developments affected the church's comprehension of its reason for existence. Like the Constantinian shift, the Cartesian and Protestant shifts had an arguably unfortunate impact on the church's understanding of itself, and ultimately its understanding of God.

REFORMATION AND REASON

As the prime mover of Christendom in the centuries following the demise of the Roman Empire, the Roman church took a leading role in not only providing guidance to various civil authorities but at times directing them as well. While the chief goal of the leaders of what was to become the Protestant Reformation certainly had ecclesial correction in mind, their efforts had political implications as well.

Martin Luther maintained that Christians lived simultaneously under two governances, one temporal and the other spiritual. He acknowledged the validity of coercive power, given by God to secular entities for maintaining peace. The church was to avoid entanglements with politics since that was the domain of coercive power. The church's influence was instead based on persuasion by the Word of God. The church's domain was spiritual, the government's domain was temporal, and the former was subject to the latter. This, in effect meant that the church increasingly saw to the disposition of the souls of members, while secular authorities dealt with the body and thus the outward life of these same members.[34]

Where Luther argued for restraint on the part of Christians in dealing with the governmental realm, Calvin maintained a more active stance. Politics should be an active realm of activity for Christians, who should seek to reform worldly political entities.[35] His inclination to a "stern biblical morality" meant that Calvin was more inclined to produce change in society, including attempts

34. Cavanaugh, *Theopolitical Imagination*, 23–24.
35. Noll, *One Nation Under God*, 21.

to transform local and national government.[36] Lutherans were relatively peaceful compared to "the government-toppling cadres issuing from Geneva."[37]

For all of the worth of the Reformation, it was nonetheless fraught with its own dangers. Prior to the sixteenth century, ecclesial power was assumed to dominate the other major dimension of public life, civil power. "[A]lthough the institutional arrangements that emerged in the West [by virtue of Constantinianism and Christendom] did entangle the church's eschatological mission within the idolatrous presumptions of imperial power, they did have their advantages when compared with subsequent developments in the post-Reformation era."[38] The Christendom concept of a more or less single body (with ecclesial and civil dimensions organically unified) remained into the sixteenth century. However, due to the rapidly changing social and political structures that developed in territories mapped around the reformers' influence, dominance became inverted to the civil authority. This inversion made possible the eventual elimination of the church as alternative *polis* from the public realm.[39]

Distinctions such as those made by Luther paved the way for the struggle between church and civil authority by allowing the latter an open field. Calvin's approach meant that challenges to other ecclesial authorities frequently went hand-in-hand with challenges to civil authority producing predictable civil responses. As the state rose in power, so did its need to control the church in whatever manifestations present within the state's territory. The splintering of the Christian faith into Roman Catholic and various Protestant bodies ultimately evolved into wars, ostensibly over the influence of religious groups. What was at stake in the so-called Wars of Religion "was the creation of religion as a set of privately

36. Graham, *The Constructive Revolutionary*, 20–21.
37. Ibid.
38. Harvey, *Another City*, 78.
39. Cavanaugh, *Theopolitical Imagination*, 23–24.

held beliefs without direct political relevance."[40] What appeared to be in-fighting among various factions of the church made the way clear for the birth of the nation-state, which opportunistically sought sovereignty over all church bodies. However, the nation-state was forced into the role of referee in attempts to diminish these wars.

Loyalty to civil authority became primary as religion was relegated to an internal, personal issue. As long as the individual acted in public ways that implied allegiance to the state above devotion to the church, the person was granted whatever rights the government happen to accord to its citizens. The church's influence diminished as faith was pushed from the public sphere, and the demands of the nation-state overshadowed all others. In essence, the authority of the church was employed even more intently toward the sustenance of the nation-state.

Another significant shift occurring essentially concurrently to the Reformation was a philosophical transformation traceable to the work of René Descartes. A French philosopher and mathematician, he is noted as one of the principal architects of the modern age. According to Descartes, the institutions and practices of the inherited society were determined to be tenuous at best. Humankind was more reasonable and capable of ordering life than were the religions, empires, and sciences of the seventeenth century. Four aspects of Descartes' systematic re-imagining of the world contributed to this ongoing shift.

First was an extreme "desire to overcome fate, or at least to drastically limit the role it plays in human affairs."[41] Humanity was deemed capable of determining all aspects of its own future, a concept that represented an attempt by man to leave the anachronistic forces of religion behind and take on the divine mantle.

Next was the conceptualizing of all things external to the human soul as things to be "conquered, possessed, controlled, and

40. Ibid., 26.
41. Harvey, *Another City*, 97.

colonized."[42] Humankind was master of creation, with all its dimensions existing for the taking, ultimately to be manipulated to serve humankind's values and purposes.

A third dimension of Cartesian invention loosed humankind from Jewish and Christian moorings as the narrative by which to understand the world—its source, meaning, and end—was attributable to "a sort of omnipotent novelist."[43] Yet this loosening was not complete, for the idea of a universal story even with Jewish and Christian overtones still held some vague validity.

The fourth concept attending to the work at hand is the redefinition of the notion of secular. Prior to the seventeenth century the Latin *saeculum* referred to a particular time rather than a space or realm distinct from religious or sacred, in particular the time between the fall and the eschaton. Under Descartes and his disciples, *saeculum*—secular—came to refer to a space in the world over which humans, not God, were sovereign. Freedom from God and the relationships designed by God was necessary, now that the finite was isolated from connection with the infinite.[44]

The stage was set for the Enlightenment, and even more significant challenges to the church's understanding of God and *missio Dei*. Also known as the Age of Reason, the Enlightenment represented a blossoming of the philosophical constructions begun by Descartes, among others. Immanuel Kant viewed the Enlightenment as "humanity's coming of age . . . [and] the emergence from the immaturity that caused human beings to rely on such external authorities as the Bible, the church, and the state to tell them what to think and what to do."[45] The Enlightenment laid the foundation for the modern era as barriers to progress disappeared to allow man freedom to take full responsibility for individual fulfillment. Communal commitments were taken to be

42. Ibid., 99.
43. Ibid., 102.
44. Ibid., 104–105.
45. Brown, *The Rise of Western Christendom*, 377.

hindrances to personal realization. Individuals entered into social contracts with other individuals, and all accepted certain restraining natural laws that allowed the interests of the majority to determine what would benefit all.

All faiths and creeds were expected to acquiesce to the demands of reason. Governments existed at the behest of those who were to be governed, not ordained by God. Christianity was determined to be divisive; a church with loyalties that transcended national borders and limited allegiance to rulers was unacceptable.[46] The so-called Wars of Religion were pretense for the rise of the modern nation-state.[47] Progressive political concepts collaborated with assaults on the foundations of a biblical Christianity.

Enlightenment thinkers were well acquainted with multiple disciplines, making it possible for them to apply reason to the rapidly expanding Western civilization. Among many Enlightenment thinkers, Hobbes, Locke, Rousseau, and Voltaire were particularly influential in redefining the relationship between the state and the Christianity. All sought to tame the church for the sake of unity.

Hobbes sought to unite the state and the church, and the kingdom of God had its own realm within the commonwealth. There was no need for a transnational church since each state could claim its own self-contained religious identity. Locke, who was agnostic, encouraged religious pluralism, and religion was an interior matter for the individual. Rousseau sought to produce a civil religion that would foster a primary loyalty of the citizen to the state. Religious diversity was useful to the state by isolating factions of the church from one another. Worship was an inward matter and allowed in public gatherings as long as it did not interfere with the duties and

---

46. "Christianity produces divisions within the state body precisely because it has pretensions to be a body which transcends state boundaries." Cavanaugh, *Theopolitical Imagination*, 38.

47. The Wars of Religion were not mere conflicts between Catholics and Protestants, but "were fought largely for the aggrandizement of the emerging state over the decaying remnants of the medieval ecclesial order." Ibid., 22.

obligations of civil obedience. Voltaire joined Rousseau in declination of the institutional church, i.e., Christendom.

The Age of Reason effectively established the conceptual framework for reality in the burgeoning modern world. First, the modern nation-state was accepted as sovereign over all aspects of life, including the church and religion. Second, the meaning of religion was transformed, making it a matter of personal choice. Belief was a private matter simply to be reinforced as such by church and worship, which in turn bolstered the citizen in his or her support of the nation-state. Third, life was dichotomized into secular and sacred realms, with the secular being accepted as public and principal and the sacred as internal and subordinate. Fourth, the concepts of private and public space were established, relegating faith and religion to the private sphere, and the public being defined as the political sphere with all control over social, economic, and national matters for the good and protection of the citizens. Fifth, the temporal and eternal were disjoined from one another. Sixth, life was dissected further into mystical and physical aspects. These constructs effectively domesticated the church.[48]

In bold, broad strokes, the church came under the dominance of the modern nation-state. The leaders of these new political entities were free to "direct doctrinal conflicts to serve secular ends."[49] Such manipulation was possible due to the appearance of a state religion that replaced the institutional church, whose belief systems had been effectively redirected for other purposes. Christian identity now had little to do with "practices and virtues that give sense and direction to one's interaction with the world"[50] from a biblical perspective. Instead, virtues and practices focused on good citizenry, and the public role of the individual as citizen of the nation took precedence. "What emerged was our current circumstance of churches in principle tied to one another, but

48. Ibid., 39, 42.
49. Ibid., 42.
50. Ibid., 90.

in practice identifying their religious duties as coterminous with those of 'their' nation-states or local political/ethnic authorities."[51]

In spite of the centuries-long influence of Christendom (or perhaps as a result of it), the Western cultural landscape changed dramatically in the eighteenth century as the church was removed from its dominant role. The declining influence of theology and faith, combined with a rising and optimistic humanism, paved the way for the redefinition of God in terms more suited to a world dominated by rational and autonomous individuals. Revealed religion (based on Scripture) gave way to a focus on natural religion (truth accessible to humans through reason). Religion could teach humans about God without requiring that they engage in true worship.[52]

History has a way of weaving a variety of seemingly unrelated movements and endeavors into an intriguing fabric. The results are generally unintentional and unpredictable, and would probably be surprising to the groups and individuals involved. The church had certainly developed an affinity for organization prior to the Constantinian shift. After the fourth century, however, the overt institutionalism and nationalism that came to characterize much of the church's engagement with its world would likely have been shocking to first or even second century Christ-followers. The confluence of Christendom, the Reformation, and the Age of Reason may have redefined the church, but the waves of change in humanity's self-conception created durable connections among religion, politics, and philosophy. The *ekklesia* born into the exhilaration of Christ's triumphant resurrection and ascension learned different lessons about triumph—those formed in the image of human agendas with increasingly fewer ties to the kingdom of God's reign in Christ. The resulting triumphalism traded truths that could easily become embedded in the rising humanist tide.

51. Budde, "Selling America, Restricting the Church," 80.
52. Cavanaugh, *Theopolitical Imagination*, 33–34.

The resulting reasonable religion known as *deism* suited the needs of this triumphalism perfectly.

Religion as a concept served the needs of the burgeoning nation-state rather well. The church was tamed, and its message became fodder for use by the state. The concept of religion made theologically compelling through deism marginalized the gospel, as the Christian's loyalty to the state could be justified under the guise of proper devotion to God.[53] The influence of revealed religion waned. Its insistence on orthodoxy made strenuous demands that were not in keeping with a population of autonomous, reasonable, and progressing individuals. Such individuals were empowered to seek their own good, even at the expense of the community. The authority of Scripture and the church were passé. Christianity was welcome at the new table as long as it was willing to fit itself into the new humanity. The "religion of reason" had staked its claim; orthodox Christianity was surely an aberration of what it was intended to be in the first place.

53. Ibid., 112.

4

Nationalism Part 2:
A God for a New World

THE UPSTART colonies in North America were prime territory for the influx of these new ideas. These new-world citizens were prepared to form a new way of living together. The United States of America was a product of the Enlightenment, and the nation's Constitution contains a long list of Enlightenment affirmations.

Choosing an understanding of God that would fit into the experiment of a new form of government was a vital step in creating this new world. It was being shaped in the mold of a democratic liberalism, which, in good Age of Reason form, propounded individualism, human (and thus, personal as opposed to public or corporate) rights, property rights, and a new influence on the horizon—capitalism.[1] This enterprise was made easier by the milieu created by dynamic new forces working in concert with one another, rather than in contradiction. Essentially, "Protestantism and enlightenment were two faces of the same happy family."[2]

The nation's identity was forged in the midst of new philosophical and ethical foundations for civic polity and personal piety. Within fifty years of the nation's founding, "the synthesis of evangelicalism, republicanism, and common sense had become, not only the most powerful value system in the nation, but also

1. Herbert, *Religion and Civil Society*, 104.
2. May, *The Enlightenment in America*, 3.

the most powerful value system defining the nation."[3] The new republic made strong efforts to insure religious freedom. Yet the nation-state took primacy over ecclesial entities, ultimately requiring an accommodationist stance by the numerous denominations vying for a place in the new society. In response to this burgeoning new-world nationalism, "Protestant believers actively embraced republican ideals, emphases, habits of thought, and linguistic conventions, and they did so by folding them into their traditional theologies."[4] This gave birth to a uniquely American religious philosophy—"Theistic common sense."[5] The result was not just a distinctly American God, but a distinctly American form of Christianity that arguably still casts its shadow over the church (and the globe) today. "The startling reversal in which America's religious leaders took up the language of republicanism was the most important ideological development for the future of theology in the United States."[6]

Born in the ferment following the arguably erroneously identified Wars of Religion, the new nation founded in the American colonies would continue the process of distancing the church from its original identity. The nation-state replaced ecclesial authority as the arbiter of the source, meaning, and end of all things, and became the guarantor for the protection of the newly recognized rights. Constitutional toleration of religious belief in any number of forms (including no religious belief) was one of the crowning jewels of liberal democracy as instituted in the United States (U.S.). This toleration, again guaranteed by the liberal democratic nation-state Constitutionally exemplified in this new collective, came with a heavy cost, however. The secular realm of government was primary, and the sacred realm of the church was secondary at best. Toleration made it possible for diverse expressions of the Christian

3. Noll, *America's God*, 14.
4. Ibid., 73.
5. Ibid., 93.
6. Ibid.

faith to coexist. "[O]nce Christians are made to chant 'We have no king but Caesar,' it is really a matter of indifference to the sovereign whether there be one religion or many."[7] As the domain of public policy toward religion, toleration then became "the tool through which the church [was] divided and conquered."[8]

The deistic God of the Age of Reason was ideal for this enterprise. This God was reasonable since by use of humankind's intuitive reasoning God could be understood and described. Faith was not required to attain knowledge of this God. This was the God of nature—who ordered the universe and all natural things into a logical system of existence. This God allowed human persons to decide what was right in their own estimation based on reason and nature. This God promoted harmony through creation; this was God's primary means of giving life and sustenance to humanity. This, too, was the God of progress whose nature and harmony and gifting of humankind to be reasonable made it possible for life in the world to advance on an unlimited scale.

This God became America's God, but it is not quite the God as known through the story of ancient Israel and in the person of Jesus Christ. This God would produce American Christians who were well-schooled in the Enlightenment's "social philosophy . . . predicated on self-interest and property."[9] Like their early enlightened predecessors, these Christians tended to value their individuality at the expense of communal interactions. These highly religious individuals became over time, willing to accept the concept that other persons may choose to follow a different understanding of truth, particularly under the influence of postmodernism. They tended to value the sense of harmony produced by natural laws in the universe above the direction of Holy Spirit. They would pursue the Enlightenment concepts of autonomy and progress in this world.

7. Cavanaugh, *Theopolitical Imagination*, 40.
8. Ibid.
9. Sawyer, *The Church on the Margins*, 34.

DEISTIC DYNAMIC

While this distinctly American God was deistic[10] in formulation, it was more than the watchmaker God described by the original Enlightenment thinkers. This deistic God had a particular concern for America, people led by God from Europe "to establish a new sort of social order that shall be a light unto all nations."[11] The use of biblical imagery and metaphor to describe America became, and remains, common practice. The rising American scene was fertile for this cross-pollination of theology and reason.

America's particular form of Enlightenment-based religious practice is legally recognized as *ceremonial deism*. Eugene Rostow introduced the term as a legal concept in 1962 referring to certain religious practices that became Constitutional because they have become conventional by common and repeated use and are, therefore, no longer controversial. Rostow had in mind the deist god, singular in person, and represented in the beliefs of a significant number of America's founders. This is the god that "created the universe and the laws of nature and life, but . . . does not interfere with its creation: it merely observes what happens. There are no miracles. There are no divine interventions or revelations."[12]

The Supreme Court of the United States has used this concept in deciding certain cases related to the establishment clause. "If a practice is customary, then even if it amounts to government endorsement of a particular religion or religious belief, it may be

---

10. Deism stood as an antithesis to orthodox Christianity. It acknowledged God as creator; this Creator, however, "established natural laws [and] then [withdrew] from the world." Deism relinquished the idea of a "biblical or personal knowledge of God." God could be best known by comprehending these natural laws, and these natural laws "in turn defined natural rights." This God was "religious," and not at all political. Ibid.

11. Bellah, *Beyond Belief*, 175.

12. Thorne, "The Tangled Web of Ceremonial Deism."

beyond the reach of the establishment clause."[13] Christmas[14] is cited as an example as is the use of the phrases "In God We Trust" on legal tender and "under God" in the pledge to the American flag. These have lost any significant religious content because of rote repetition in the public realm.

Another type of deism currently practiced in the U.S. was recently described as "Moralistic Therapeutic Deism."[15] The central elements of Moralistic Therapeutic Deism seek to instill an ethical manner of living while offering beneficial value to participants. A unique addition to the deism inherited from the eighteenth-century Enlightenment is the therapeutic character of this God, who is essentially on call for solving life's difficult issues.

This deism represents a "revisionist faith"[16] that is inconsistent with the orthodoxy understood by early followers of Christ. This deistic God has no explicit expectations of adherents. Moralistic Therapeutic Deism is defined as "a widely shared, largely apolitical, interreligious faith fostering subjective well-being and lubricating interpersonal relationships in the local public sphere."[17] This form of deism is reflected in creedal-like statements such as:[18]

1. A God exists who created and orders the world and watches over human life on earth.

2. God wants people to be good, nice, and fair to each other, as taught in the Bible and by most world religions.

3. The central goal of life is to be happy and to feel good about oneself.

---

13. Ibid.

14. "The holiday has been celebrated by so many for so long that it's no endorsement of Christianity for it to be a national holiday." Ibid.

15. Smith and Denton, *Soul Searching*, 162.

16. Ibid., 166.

17. Ibid., 169.

18. Ibid., 162–163.

4. God does not need to be particularly involved in one's life except when God is needed to resolve a problem.

5. Good people go to heaven when they die.

This is a telling summary of the beliefs of persons in the U.S. who consider themselves to be religious. It obviously bears the marks of a lack of particularity about what it means to follow God as encountered in the story of ancient Israel and in the person of Jesus Christ.[19]

Theologies such as ceremonial deism and Moralistic Therapeutic Deism reflect the Kantian view that religion is primarily purposeful for the pursuit of virtue. Virtue was merely a means of proposing that people were to be good in life. By extension of this idea, another purpose, then, of religion is to produce good people who are good citizens. Good citizens living under deism find that loyalty to nation is easily equated with religious action. The role of the religion of the American deistic God is to produce good, moral individuals who are patriotic and nationalistic in their orientation. Any allegiance beyond that is strictly up to the individual.

The American experiment created a place where people would be free to worship God under whatever theological framework they happen to choose, or gods, or even no god at all. The U.S. Constitution clearly states that the government is to establish no religion, offering its citizens freedom. The Constitutional separation of church and state is not stated specifically in those

19. The book, *Soul Searching*, is an analysis of the National Study of Youth and Religion conducted by the University of North Carolina at Chapel Hill from 2001 to 2005. While this study focused on 13–19 year olds, Smith and Denton venture to add that they believe that Moralistic Therapeutic Deism is widely practiced among religious adults in the U.S. as well. They conclude: "we have come with some confidence to believe that a significant part of Christianity in the United States is actually only tenuously Christian in any sense that is seriously connected to the actual historical Christian tradition . . . It is not so much that U.S. Christianity is being secularized. Rather more subtly, Christianity is either degenerating into a pathetic version of itself or, more significantly, Christianity is actively being colonized and displaced by quite a different religious faith." Ibid., 171.

terms in that document's text. To the extent that this principle exists in the nation's Constitution, it exists to protect the church from intrusion by the state, not to protect the state from the church. The church was not to have dominion over the government, and the government is also not intended to have dominion over the church. This separation was deemed appropriate under Christian principles, such as render unto Caesar what is Caesar's and unto God what is God's.[20] While God was allowed to be religious yet not political, the nation could be political and still be religious, albeit in a unique fashion. Hence the American form of liberal ideology allowed for "*a religious dimension to its nationalism that was secular in application*" (emphasis mine).[21] In essence, the American form of public—or civil—religion became a desacralized expression of religion, standing beyond the influence of the church in general, and of what it means to follow Christ in particular.

God is a widely used term in American civil religion, a nationalistic religion described as "a collection of beliefs, symbols, and rituals with respect to sacred things and institutionalized in a collectivity. This religion while not antithetical to and indeed sharing much in common with Christianity, was neither sectarian nor in any specific sense Christian."[22] The concept of God under this civil religion allows the invocation of God without respect to any particular interpretation of God. From Washington forward, all presidents of the U.S. have spoken of God in some way. This frequent mention of God, however, is intentionally innocuous, so much so that it is "a word that almost all Americans can accept but that means so many different things to so many people that it is almost an empty sign."[23] Under the banner of civil religion,

20. This is a commonly stated version of Jesus' statements recorded in Matt 22:21, Mark 12:17, and Luke 20:25. An exploration of this narrative is included in Chapter 4 below.

21. Horsley, *Jesus and Empire*, 148.

22. Bellah, *Beyond Belief*, 175.

23. Ibid., 170.

God becomes a symbol, yet with no particular creed to establish demands on citizens beyond those of the nation's laws.

American civil religion has made it possible for the country's narrative to bear biblical imagery and metaphor apart from biblical authority. The idea of America as a new Israel after an exodus from Europe was invoked frequently and ardently from the nation's earliest days. The concept of the American people as a chosen people of God with a special task in the world has also appeared with regularity. Washington, Jefferson, Franklin, and even Lincoln held these concepts to be true, and used them in spoken as well as written communication.

No doubt America's civil religion has proved valuable in creating the national narrative since it has provided some sense of common heritage and constituted something new in the world's history. "It has its own prophets, and its own martyrs, its own sacred events and sacred places, its own solemn rituals and symbols. It is concerned that America be a society as perfectly in accord with the will of God as men can make it, and a light to all the nations."[24] Such a nation is certainly likely to benefit the world.

The American national narrative, by some standards containing mythic overtones, has allowed the U.S. to lay claim to a unique blessing of God. This has given its leaders permission to claim for the nation a place in the world not unlike Israel or even the first *ekklesia*. The practiced use of "crypto-Christian language"[25] and co-opted Scripture as props for these claims presumes what amounts to messianic provenance for the nation.

While continually in dispute, the idea that the U.S. is—or is not, or should not be, or could become again—a Christian nation is rarely far from the conscious thought of many citizens.[26]

24. Ibid., 186.

25. Chapman, "Imperial Exegesis," 96.

26. A full examination of the ongoing yes-and-no disputations regarding America's identity as a Christian nation is well beyond the scope of this book, much less this single chapter. The volume of print and rhetorical argumentation is nearly staggering. A brief sampling of statements is included here.

In 1892, a Supreme Court decision outlined a series of considerations that led to the conclusion that "These, and many other matters which might be noticed, add a volume of unofficial declarations to the mass of organic utterances that this is a Christian nation." Church of the Holy Trinity v. United States 143 U.S. 471.

Justice David J. Brewer, who served on the court for the above cited case, was compelled to write a clarification regarding this very issue. "But in what sense can it be called a Christian nation? Not in the sense that Christianity is the established religion or the people are compelled in any manner to support it. On the contrary, the Constitution specifically provides that 'congress shall make no law respecting an establishment of religion or prohibiting the free exercise thereof.' Neither is it Christian in the sense that all its citizens are either in fact or in name Christians. On the contrary, all religions have free scope within its borders. Numbers of our people profess other religions, and many reject all. Nor is it Christian in the sense that a profession of Christianity is a condition of holding office or otherwise engaging in public service, or essential to recognition either politically or socially. In fact, the government as a legal organization is independent of all religions. Nevertheless, we constantly speak of this republic as a Christian nation—in fact, the leading Christian nation of the world. This popular use of the term certainly has significance." Brewer, *The United States*, 12.

Indiana Senator Albert J. Beveridge, who was also a Pulitzer Prize winning historian, made a very bold claim: "Almighty God has marked the American people as the chosen nation to finally lead in the regeneration of the world. This is the divine mission of America . . . We are the trustees of the world's progress, guardians of the righteous peace. 'Ye have been faithful over a few things; I will make you ruler over many things.'" Beveridge, "In Support of an American Empire."

President Ronald Reagan told the country that America was involved in a struggle of cosmic proportions "between right and wrong and good and evil" and that the country was "enjoined by Scripture and the Lord Jesus to oppose it [referring to the Soviet Union] with all our might." Reagan, "Remarks at the Annual Convention of the National Association of Evangelicals."

President George W. Bush made the following statements in remarks to a gathering at Ellis Island on September 11, 2002: "Ours is the cause of human dignity; freedom guided by conscience and guarded by peace. This ideal of America is the hope of all humankind. That hope drew millions to this harbor. That hope still lights our way. And the light shines in the darkness. And the darkness will not overcome it." Bush, "The President's Address to the Nation."

President Barak Obama stated in one instance that Americans "do not consider ourselves a Christian nation, or a Muslim nation, but rather a nation of citizens who are . . . bound by a set of values." In another, he remarked,

Constitutionally, the U.S. lacks resonance with the biblical use of the term *Christian*, however, which appears in Scripture as a noun used to describe followers of Christ.[27] When used as an adjective, *Christian* is open to uses that at best may be only vaguely related to Christ-following and at worst may actually be antithetical to the hoped-for biblical implications.

It has become common practice for all Americans, including those who claim to be Christian, to watch and listen for its public leaders to engage in civil religion. The language of this civil religion contains "faintly Protestant platitudes which reaffirm the religious base of American culture despite being largely void of theological significance."[28] The lack of theological meaning does not prevent, however, the cultural impact of what amounts to pious clichés. The American people are formed and shaped by such statements. One is left to wonder exactly what kind of influence people thus formed and shaped will offer in the world.

> The platitudes of America's civil religion are expected and accepted—but they are only platitudes. They have no theology, except perhaps, as Wuthnow notes, a theology of "America First." It may be that we are comfortable with them precisely because they demand nothing of us. Not only are they easily ignored by those who happen to have no religious beliefs, but

---

"Whatever we once were, we are no longer a Christian nation—at least not just" then continuing that the U.S. is also Jewish, Muslim, Hindu, Buddhist, "and a nation of nonbelievers." Eidsmoe, "Obama: America Not a Christian Nation."

Different views also receive notice. "Contrary to the claims made by some from the Religious Right, America was not founded as a Christian Nation which was then later undermined by godless liberals and humanists. Just the opposite is the case, actually. The Constitution is a godless document and the government of the United States was set up as a formally secular institution. It has, however, been undermined by well-meaning Christians who have sought to subvert its secular principles and framework for the sake of this or that 'good cause,' usually in the interest of promoting this or that religious doctrine." Cline, "America a Christian Nation."

27. Acts 11:26, 26:28; 1 Pet 4:16.

28. Gedicks, "The Religious, the Secular, and the Antithetical," 113, 122.

they make virtually no demands on the consciences of those who do. God is thanked for the success of an enterprise recently completed or asked to sanctify one not yet fully begun. God is asked to bless the nation, its people, and its leaders. But nobody, in the civil religion, is asked to do anything for God.[29]

Consider the following summary of civil religion in light of the influences of Constantinianism, Christendom, the Reformation, and the Age of Reason. Civil religion develops as a nation-state seeks validation from the church or prevailing religious order for its establishment, protection, sustenance, and ambitions. It propagates itself through a cross-pollination of the stories, symbols, and celebrations of the church and nation-state. This cross-pollination exerts an arguably dubious influence on the church, and results in the conception of an on-going history of the nation-state with the character of sacrosanct myth. In order for civil religion to flourish, the willing participation of the church or prevailing religious order is necessary at some level.

The following observations delineate some characteristics of the interfacing of a nation-state and the church and its gospel under the influence of a civil religion:

- The nation-state will generally act in ways that presume that the goals and agendas of the nation-state and the church are, at least to some extent, co-terminus.

- The church will generally act in ways that acknowledge that the goals and agendas of the church and nation-state are not co-terminus, but deem the perceived advantages to the church's opportunity to present the gospel are worth the risk of entanglement.

- The nation-state will exercise its authority so that its agenda will trump the agenda of the gospel; the gospel will be subordinated to the nation-state's agenda.

29. Carter, *The Culture of Disbelief*, 51–52.

- The nation-state will seek to define transcendence and ultimacy in a way that, while integrating themes that appear consistent with the gospel, is bent toward the health, sustenance, and ambitions of the nation-state.

- The nation-state will always co-opt and even abuse the gospel to support its own ends.

- The nation-state will encourage the existence and even freedom of the church to the extent that the church complies with the means and ends of the nation-state.

- The nation-state will presume that the church's complicity implies support for its policies, including whatever coercive means the nation-state determines are necessary to maintain its security and future.

- Any complicity on the part of the church with the nation-state will generate dissonance between the church and the gospel; while this may begin subtly, this dissonance will intensify, eroding the church's concept of its core identity and mission.

- The church that is faithful to the gospel will generally represent a dissenting voice to the demands of the nation-state.

- The gospel's intent will, therefore, be perceived as a threat to the nation-state.

- The church will face the temptation to use statecraft as its means of validating its voice and message in the public square. This use of statecraft will amount to an appropriation of worldly principalities and powers.

Entanglements as noted above are not a matter of interchanges between something that is spiritual (faith) and another thing that is not (nation). Indeed nationalism breeds a unique spiritual quality all its own. First century Christians experienced this firsthand. The pagan temples throughout Rome housed numerous statues dedicated to the gods—Caesar among them. "What people in the world of the Bible experienced as and called 'principalities and powers' was in fact the actual spirituality at the center of the political, economic, and cultural institutions of their day."[30] This spiritual quality of nationalistic devotion is just as prevalent in our own day, and is precisely the reason why religious and civic pieties make such quick, easy, and—for the gospel—risky partners.

In spite of the temptations to value civil religion as an opportunity for leveraging the power of the state for the purposes of the gospel, the danger is readily apparent. The church under fourth-century Roman rule could not have foreseen the implications of the empire's acceptance and ultimate legalization. The church in the twenty-first century has as much or more reason to be cautious, yet with the value of hindsight not afforded Christ's followers centuries earlier. There is, however, a unique opportunity for faithfulness to the gospel embedded in the American civil landscape. It has nothing to do with a vision of America as a Christian nation.

The pluralistic society of American democratic capitalism is distinct from all other traditionalist or socialist societies.[31] These other societal forms enforce some unified framework defining ultimate goodness and truth. These systems exercise one collective authority over all powers within the society, whether they be political, economic, or moral-cultural. This is not so in America, since no single "sacred canopy"[32] calls to order the political, economic, and moral-cultural dimensions of this society.

This lack of a sacred canopy is intentional, leaving an "empty shrine"[33] at the spiritual core of any pluralistic society, including that of the U.S. The emptiness of this shrine makes it possible for all consciences, free of the constraints of an enforced core, to claim transcendence. Within this empty shrine, "God" may be acknowl-

---

30. Wink, *The Powers that Be*, 24.
31. Novak, *The Spirit of Democratic Capitalism*, 49.
32. Ibid.
33. Ibid., 53.

edged. Yet no person or entity may define the identity, content, or character of "God" for any other person or entity.

Attempts to arrange a pluralistic society around one vision of social order create a *command* society—one in which a single vision of good is imposed on all participants.[34] The command compels the society to comply. Such a society is not then pluralistic, and is likely to demean the personhood and conscience of many if not all citizens.

All religious leaders hold the belief that their vision for society is reality. The demands of competition with other symbols and ideas of different realities are, however, deemed by some to be unmanageable. Religious leaders can be lured into crafting, even by coercive means, their society into one based on their vision, their reality. Yet "Respect for the transcendence of God and for full freedom of conscience—respect for the common human wandering in darkness—is better served . . . even in Christian and Jewish terms, by the reverential emptiness at the heart of pluralism than by a socially imposed vision of the good."[35]

Christian symbols and themes are best when not used in attempts to command the system. Such attempts are likely to do damage to the society at large and will certainly be dangerous for the integrity of Christian faith. The imposition of faith on any society, American or not, by command—coercion—is to employ precisely the strategy that produced the Crusades under Christendom. The mutual conflict of ideas and values and institutions in American pluralistic society will inhibit such a centering of Christianity in this society. Yet such a society is to be valued, not demeaned.

Herein lays the opportunity for the church as the body of Christ. A society that protects the empty shrine is precisely the kind of culture within which followers of Christ acting communally as alternative *polis* can, and should, flourish. If any religious paradigm is allowed dominance over others, none are safe from

34. Ibid., 67.
35. Ibid., 68.

encroachment—even the dominant paradigm. The holiness of the triune God and the veracity of the gospel are true regardless of the level of freedom or restraint present in the society within which the church exists. The mission to which God calls Christians and for which Christ begat the church is best served by freedom to worship and witness faithfully. Even if the church is pressed to the margins of society or even underground, it is still more valuable as an alternative *polis* than if it seeks to command the participation of persons within the society who are outside the faith.

Arguably, an empty shrine in such a society may not remain empty for long. Various formulations of God or gods or no god at all may seek to claim the intentionally unoccupied center. The nation itself would surely be among contenders for the spot, calling for reverential treatment nigh unto high religiosity. Patriotic celebrations, even containing civil religious practices, are certainly appropriate in the broader culture. Such nationalistic rites have a place in the larger society, especially when that society allows citizens freedom to seek or ignore God. In the great pluralist tradition these events at times employ "God language" and possibly even biblical ideas, all with no intention of doing so for necessarily religious purposes. Yet bringing patriotic rituals into the worship life of the church crosses a perilous threshold since "All worship outside the worship of God through Christ Jesus is idolatrous."[36] It would be a mistake to confuse nationalistic liturgical festivities with biblical faith and Christological worship.

There is no doubt that Christ-followers in America enjoy the opportunity provided by a pluralistic society to worship faithfully. Followers of Christ may not be compelled to accept any other interpretation of "God" than what they choose. They likewise have no right to command-by-might their understanding of God in Christ upon any other persons or groups who choose otherwise. There is Constitutional guarantee for both. In effect, as Christ-followers participate in protecting the empty shrine from all chal-

36. Best, *Unceasing Worship*, 17.

70

lengers, including the state, they guard their own rights as well as the rights of others. That does not make it proper, however, for congregations of Christ-followers to incorporate within their worship symbols and rituals of the nation's civil religious practice that signify a "God" which is not explicitly identified as God in Christ. Such activities represent an attempt to integrate the worship of gods that are not the holy triune God. A mixing of this sort may offer a view of reality that is only consonant with Scripture in a vague manner. Hence caution is required:

> [these practices] may well be symptoms of the attempt which is possible in so many forms to incorporate that which is alien in other prophecies into what is proper to that of Jesus Christ. If these prophecies are prepared for this—and sooner or later they will make an open bid for sole dominion—the prophecy of Jesus Christ asks to be excused and avoids such incorpora tion. If it is subjected to such combinations, the living Lord Jesus and His Word depart, and all that usually remains is the suspiciously loud but empty utterance of the familiar name of this Prophet. "No one can serve two masters" (Mt. 6[24]). No man can serve both the one Word of God called Jesus Christ and other divine words.[37]

Scripture seems clear in recording the directives of the triune God: "you shall worship no other god, because the LORD, whose name is Jealous, is a jealous God."[38] Holy God steadfastly resists involvement in liturgical endeavors in which God is expected to receive accolades alongside other persons or entities—regardless of how worshipful those endeavors are presumed to be. Speaking through the prophet Isaiah, God said: "I am the LORD, that is my name; my glory I give to no other, nor my praise to idols."[39]

The moral-cultural constructions begun under Constantinianism and nurtured to full bloom in Christendom represent a traditionalist society, one in which Christianity held a centering and

37. Barth, *Church Dogmatics* IV.3.1, 102.
38. Exod 34:14.
39. Isa 42:8; c.f., 48:11.

commanding role. The Protestant Reformation may have diminished that centering and commanding role. Yet its replacement of the institutional church with other forms of institutionalism did little to restore the vibrancy of the early Christ-following *ekklesia*. The Enlightenment made it difficult for any institutionalized form of Christendom-model church to function, yet may have paved the way for the gospel's most profound opportunity for influence in the world since before Constantine. The church's continued attempts at Christendom in the United States have likely prevented the church from seizing the opportunity offered by the pluralism of democratic capitalism.

EMPIRE REVISITED

Metaphorical expressions categorizing the United States as a new Israel were common in the nation's early history. Yet the symbolism of chosen people living in a land flowing with good things is not the only comparison that has drawn attention. Similarities between the U.S. and the Roman Empire have surfaced as well. Like Rome, America has seemed "destined to bring civilization, law, and order to the whole world."[40] One could certainly make a case for the perception that America has acted, even if unintentionally, as an empire. Characteristics common to empires include systemic centralizations of power, socioeconomic and military control often expressed in oppressive economics, powerful myths (*Pax Romana* becomes *Pax Americana*), and imperial images that capture people's imagination.[41]

While not following the practices of Euro-imperialism that preceded its rise to world-wide influence, identifying America as an imperial power, though arguable, is pertinent. As practiced on the continent, manifest destiny—claiming continental sovereignty under the providence of God's blessing—made the extension of

40. Horsley, *Jesus and Empire*, 137.
41. Walsh and Keesmaat, *Colossians Remixed*, 58–63.

borders and influence a noble act and even a sectarian duty, regardless of the cost required of some continental inhabitants or the fragility of abundant natural resources.

The expansion of American style democracy has not been limited to American boundaries. While colonialism may have been more overt in its objectives, America's extension of its own way of governing the populace has been freely and, at times insistently, offered on virtually every continent for the benefit of people everywhere. World peace and prosperity were manifest in America's destiny as it responded to providence's call to spread the news.

American citizens in general, however, tend to eschew any thoughts of an American empire. Along with the late twentieth-century ascendance of the U.S. as the world's single super power came the "myth of the *reluctant* super power" (emphasis mine).[42] Accordingly, if America has prospered it is not what America chose but is owing to the providence of the Creator. The world would benefit, then, because America has had this mantle of peace and prosperity thrust upon it. It is in part this willingness to see all American action and policy as inherently positive that creates for the church in America a unique challenge.

Imperialism has a unique character that reveals the intentions of any imperialist actor. "Imperialism is the name we give to other people's proposals for human unity."[43] Unity among humanity is certainly to be valued and is, no doubt, consistent with the Judeo-Christian heritage. It is also one example of a Christian principle present in American civil religion appearing to be consistent with the gospel, yet ultimately lacking the true imprint of the reign of God in Christ.

One of the foundational ideals of democratic liberalism is the essential equality of all humans. Yet "every proposal for human unity that does not specify the center around which that unity is to be created, necessarily has the will, the vision, the beliefs of the

42. Bacevich, *American Empire*, 7.
43. Newbigin, *The Gospel in a Pluralist Society*, 123.

proposer as its implied center."[44] While "God" is obliquely repre-sented in America's founding documents, God in Christ is dis-tinctly absent. Hence, even Christ-followers who live in America cannot assume that an American proposal for human unity is truly Christian, since that unity does not expressly claim to be found in Christ. It follows, then, that the will, vision, and beliefs of the proposer lay at the center of the proposal—the proposer being the United States of America. That does not make such a proposal nec-essarily wrong since a common good could possibly still be served. It must be understood, however, that minus a center in Christ such a proposal is not truly representative of the biblical gospel. It can-not, therefore, be equated with *missio Dei*.

Any claims to the role of the United States as the bearer of the reign of God in the world must be roundly denied. Even if the U.S. were to become a constitutionally mandated Christian nation, this would still be true. That role has been reserved by the triune God for *ekklesia*—the community of the followers of Christ.

Once American civil religion trumps the church in such matters, religious legitimation for nationalistic imperialism can-not be far behind. A civil religion that is Christian in principle, but not truly Christ-following in action, can all too easily claim God's imprimatur for the nation's attempts at global hegemony—political, economic, or otherwise. In such a scheme, claims may be made that "God inhabits . . . nationalism or capitalism or a myriad of other 'isms,' each of which seems to its proponents to be in-vested with divine force and authority."[45] It would not be difficult to detect such vesting in consumerism, materialism, transnational globalism, or even racism. Ambiguity about God's identity in civil religion makes it possible for these and other "isms" to insinuate themselves into virtually any religious practice, placing the church's attempts at faithfulness in worship at risk.[46] Such presumption is

44. Ibid.

45. Brueggemann, *Worship in Ancient Israel*, 76.

46. "This combining of the Word of Jesus Christ with the authority and

not likely to bother the "God" of civil religion, this "God" being a somewhat empty representation due to over-use and a lack of specificity. To suppose that the triune God of Scripture revealed in Jesus Christ might honor such an ideology requires haughtiness inconsistent with biblical standards of humility, faith, and truth.

The result of the influences cited above is that worldly political entities "assume that the main political significance of the church lies in assisting the secular state in its presumption to make a better world for its citizens."[47] In far too many cases, the church has accepted those presumptions as normative. Clearly these assumptions have had an enormous impact on the church in the U.S. from the earliest moments of the nation's history. While ostensibly providing a platform for the free expression of the Christian gospel, the arrangement has allowed for an entwining of nationalistic intentions that has dampened the clarity of the gospel.

Empire has always been one of the most seductive idolatries facing the people of God.[48] Triumphalism and nationalism are characteristics of empire, both of which are aimed at sustaining the viability of the realm. The primary impulse of empire is always self-preservation. It is natural that any nation will seek its own safety and sustenance; it will do so by virtually any means necessary. Christendom learned the lessons of empire well, and

---

context of other supposed revelations and truths of God has been and is the weak point, revealed already in the *gnosis* attacked in the New Testament, at almost every point in the history of the Christian church. The prophecy of Jesus Christ has never been flatly denied, but fresh attempts have continually been made to list it with other principles, ideas and forces (and their prophecy) which are also regarded and lauded as divine, restricting its authority to what it can signify in co-ordination with them, and therefore to what remains when their authority is also granted." Barth, *Church Dogmatics* IV.3.1, 102.

47. Hauerwas and Willimon, *Resident Aliens*, 156.

48. Babylon, Tyre, and Rome all held great wealth and influence at the height of their respective imperial existences. They exhibited militaristic imperialism as well. All three are prominently featured in the Revelation to John, which, among other things, pre-images the dismissal of all worldly empires and the triumph of God's Lamb establishing God's reign on the earth.

practiced a debatably worldly state-craft along with its attempts to extend the gospel around the globe.

Worldly nationalism is a dangerous practice for the church. The inclination of nationalism to tell a self-justifying narrative tends to diminish the full truth of the gospel. Nationalism concerns itself with matters that, while possibly appearing similar to the gospel, ultimately are less than the gospel. "Nationalism . . . ought to be seen as a sectarian heresy in conflict with the universality of the Christian gospel and God's construction of a new people from all peoples and nations, and whose allegiance is to the kingdom of God rather than to the fragmented lesser powers of the modern state system."[49]

Nationalism is a well-disciplined skill of the world's statist entities. Its propensity for defending its territory and citizenry, with aggression if necessary, establishes its bias and makes its methodology clear. Self-justifying narratives are common, making it possible to "establish a patriotic religion at the heart of the state [that] gives divine sanction to the nation's imperialism."[50] The goals of endorsement via such partisan creeds place the state at the center of all things that matter, inviting idolatrous devotion.

Because the ultimate commitments of worldly nation-states are not the gospel itself, a nation-state's agenda will never clearly be consonant with the agenda to which the church is called, namely *missio Dei*. Since the first century, nation-states have proved their inability to participate in the church's prime distinguishing characteristic—its commitment to follow Christ. This is not an inconsequential commitment: "That which makes the church 'radical' and forever 'new' is . . . that the church knows Jesus whereas the world does not."[51] A failure of the church to allow its radical nature to shine on this one count will likely lead to additional compromises.

---

49. Budde, "Selling America, Restricting the Church," 81.
50. Ibid., 56.
51. Hauerwas and Willimon, *Resident Aliens*, 28.

The church in America lives in the shadow of the legacy of empire, triumphalism, and nationalism. Subsequently it faces the question: *Does the employment of nationalistic symbols, themes, and celebrations in the worship life of congregations strengthen or weaken the church's allegiance to God's reign in Christ?* While the body of Christ in this country certainly benefits from Constitutional freedoms, the answer to this question is not necessarily an easy one. Living out the gospel in a pluralist society requires deft thinking and constant caution. The very freedoms that guarantee the right of assembly also make easy partners of religion and politics in spite of the oft-cited separation of church and state.

The founding narrative and on-going saga of this host nation lacks complete fidelity to the whole of the biblical record, even though certain biblical ideals are embedded in it. The inclusion of this nation's story in the worship gatherings of Christ's followers allows what can be interpreted as an alien narrative to influence the life of the church. The demands of nationalism will always ultimately conflict with the gospel of God in Christ, creating an identity crisis for the church in its attempts to be faithful. Such a crisis will arise because of "an understanding or interpretation of Christianity determined by . . . membership in a population or community, other than the church, that becomes critical for [the church's] self-understanding and identity and purports to have a special and necessary word for the church in addition to or alternative to the word of the biblically attested Jesus."[52] Regardless of how necessary or special a word may appear to be for the church, if it is "in addition to or alternative to the word of the biblically attested Jesus," it must be approached with great vigilance, and disallowed if found less than faithful to God's Word to God's people in Christ.

When the church allows nationalistic influences within its worship—the primary identity-making practice of the church— it allows the nation-state a hand in shaping the church's identity.

52. Osborn, *The Barmen Declaration*, 45.

Once nationalism has become an element of the church's identity, the church also becomes vulnerable to that nation's partisan politics. The politics of worldly nations are rarely if ever fully consonant with the politics of the reign of God. Under the influence of nationalism, the church's ability to prophetically critique the state is limited if not completely abandoned.

Jesus located himself squarely in this prophetic tradition when he voiced Isaiah, "My house will be called *a house of prayer for all nations* (emphasis mine)."[53] The church is hard-pressed to live up to that high-calling when it gathers under the banner of a single nation—even one that allows the free exercise of religious practice. The Constitution of the U.S. guarantees freedom of religion to all citizens, wonderful indeed but temporal at best. In Christ, however, God's people are called to greater eternal mandates, the demands (and the limits contained within those demands) of which supersede even the freedoms of this nation.

The biblical record is consistent and clear: Faithfulness in worship requires commitment, and commitment requires choices. The choices required by the distinctions highlighted above are as necessary as they are difficult. The witness of the church will only be as powerful as its choices are consistent with the clear demands of honoring God in Christ, and "A church that is not 'against the world' in fundamental ways has nothing worth saying to and for the world."[54]

53. Isa 56:7; Mark 11:17.
54. Yoder, *Body Politics*, 78.

5

The Miscalculations of Liturgical Collusion

WORSHIP IS the prime identity-creating practice of the church. It is the constituting activity, repeated habitually for the sake of clarity, which discloses God in Christ as the source, character, meaning, and end of the church. By faithfulness in worship, the church declares its singular allegiance to God. In worshiping faithfully, the church also withholds devotion from all other claimants. By faithfulness in worship, the church denies the right to any other entity to establish or even define its communal self. Faithful worship becomes an exercise in naming and resisting various idolatries that confront the church as a body, and so too for its members as persons.

God's incarnation in Christ is an eternity-changing provocation on the part of the triune God. In Christ, God acts against the world yet on behalf of all persons and creation itself. Christ's followers are called to do what prevailing cultural and societal configurations cannot and will not do—exclusively worship God as encountered in the story of ancient Israel and in the person of Jesus as Messiah. Jesus exposes his followers to a political scenario that stands in contrast to all of the world's efforts at enduring political expertise. Therefore, any claim of political demeanor for the church expressed in its worship requires an accurate reflection of the political character of Jesus' life, teachings, and ministry.

If, as some claim, Jesus has no political bearing then *ekklesia* has no business attempting any political venture on Jesus' behalf. *Ekklesia's* attempts at any scheme beyond the purview of Christ in any time or place are doomed from the outset. Others may claim that Jesus does embody particular political views, which can be expressed adequately through some worldly political design or partisan intrigues within such designs. Such a claim, that bypasses Christ's followers as *ekklesia* and his chosen representatives, is in error. If *ekklesia* allows such schemes to stand by neglecting any dimension of the revelation of God in Christ, it becomes unfaithful.

The notion that Jesus was only interested in spiritual things may leave the impression that the religion of Jesus is chiefly about the inner person. If, by such reasoning, Jesus' only realm of interest was religion, then surely he has no interest in confronting the settled arrangements by which the world operates. Therefore, politics must be of one realm and religion another. It is endemic Enlightenment-based thinking that politics is only a secular affair for all citizens, equally so for those who claim to follow Christ as for those who do not.[1] If Jesus has no politics, contenders in the public "secular" realm are free to appropriate Jesus' teachings to support their own stance. Such thinking makes it possible for two Christians to find themselves on opposite sides of a partisan political issue to the point of creating disunity within the faith community. By extension, this reasoning also allows one nation-state to claim Christ's blessing for its own settled arrangements, while invalidating those of another nation-state.

The project of depoliticizing Jesus is a centuries-old process. An apolitical Jesus is a blueprint of this-worldly design, "fabricated by the attitudes of those who want to tame Christianity in order to leave the political scene free for their own views."[2] The powers that be in worldly domains have little to fear from an apolitical Christ. For example, while civil religion in America did not invent the merely religious Jesus, it certainly benefits from a Christ denied full stature. As noted above, civil religion is content with God as an indistinct deity. The radical claims of God in Christ—for sov-

1. Storkey, *Jesus and Politics*, 9.
2. Ibid.

ereignty over all of life and history and creation—makes Christ an unsuitable representative of God for any civil religion.

It is well worth noting that "in the course of its historical existence Christianity [has] repeatedly allowed itself to adopt the civil religion role."[3] Such a posture has always exacted a profound price: the denial of the fullness of Christ's claims. The world's practice of ignoring or amending the more difficult accountabilities of God's Word is a well-rehearsed proficiency. A close reading of the gospel record, however, discloses Jesus acting neither in deference to— nor in treasonous defiance of—the world's settled arrangements. Jesus Christ acts, rather, in transcendence of all of the world's settled arrangements. In so doing, he reveals an exceptional political practice—that of the coming reign of God.

WORSHIPING JESUS THE SWORD-BRINGER

In one his provocative pronouncements, Jesus said, "I have not come to bring peace, but a sword."[4] For Jewish people living under oppressive Roman rule, these words were deeply challenging. This was the same rabbi who said that those who were meek, poor in spirit, and known as peacemakers would be called blessed. The disciples to whom Jesus was speaking would have been well acquainted with the prophetic utterances of Isaiah. The anticipated Messiah would be known as the Prince of Peace, and there would be "endless peace for the throne of David and his kingdom" because of this Messiah.[5] In this instance he appeared to be speaking in contradiction of those teachings.

As subjects of Roman imperial authority, these disciples would have been well acquainted with the sword. The sword in the hands of Roman legions represented more than symbolic authority. The sword, and the hostility implied by its potential use,

3. Wannenwetsch, *Political Worship*, 148.
4. Matt 10:34.
5. Isa 9:6–7.

was intended to shatter resistance, quash insolence, and maintain order. If Jesus was the promised Messiah, his disciples were likely astounded to hear him say that he did not come to bring peace. A claim that he came with a sword would have stirred confusion among Jesus' hearers.

The storied history of Israel, combined with the expectancy for a long-foretold Messiah, created a potentially unbearable burden for anyone claiming that status. Many Jews anticipated that Messiah would bring immediate freedom from all oppression, economic want, and civil peril. Caesar was unlikely to yield sovereignty quietly. A Jewish insurrection was postponed only in anticipation of the coming of Messiah. Many of the Jews who heard Jesus, saw his miracles, and observed his every move were certain Jesus had come to fulfill that prophecy.

For centuries, the world had been an antagonistic environment for the Israelites. Their propensity for unfaithfulness to the covenantal relationship with God notwithstanding, a constant array of nations and rulers had sought to dominate the Jews, most generally with success. In spite of the people's eagerness for messianic rule, Jesus knew that the reality of his coming would not immediately realize those hopes. It was necessary for those who were following Christ to understand just how violently the world would repudiate him and his message of the reign of God. The world's rejection of Jesus would require persons to make a choice—a preference that would oblige them to walk away from other loyalties in order to follow Christ even to the point of one's own death because of that preference.

The acceptance or rejection of Christ as God's Messiah would separate people from one another. Luke also records this teaching: "Do you think I have come to bring peace to the earth?" he asks. "No, I tell you, but rather division!"[6] In this account as well as Matthew's, it is clear that even a family would experience division over the decision to follow or refuse Christ. The very notion of fa-

6. Luke 12:49–53.

milial dissection would undeniably create controversy in any society that values the strength of home and family. Jesus was anxious for his disciples to understand that "one's foes will be members of one's own household."[7] It was astonishing, to say the least, for the Prince of Peace to verbalize such a condition. It must be noted that Christ also proposes new familial ties—created through "solidarity in the work of God."[8] Jesus stated that anyone who followed him in doing the will of God would become his brother, sister, and mother.[9] Anyone who lost family by choosing Christ was promised "a hundred fold" in return.[10]

It would be natural for those who chose to follow Christ to expect antagonism from strangers. On the other hand, one might hope that a decision to follow Jesus would be celebrated by friends and family, even if they themselves chose otherwise. "It may seem incongruous to say allegiance to the gospel will lead to strife,"[11] but that is precisely Jesus' point. Peace can often be misconstrued. It is not an absence of conflict. The peace that Jesus brings is, to be sure, nonviolent. Yet the nonviolence practiced by Jesus sought conflict of a deeper sort, and even initiated it in order to reveal conflict's true source—enmity toward God. The peace that Jesus brings is "an ineffable divine reassurance within the heart of conflict."[12] Conceiving of peace in this manner required a comprehensive shift in perspective.

Jesus' intention here does not appear to be the disintegration of the family. Indeed, other scriptural injunctions entail honoring familial commitments. Respecting one's family is a good thing. Yet Jesus is making it clear that a follower must be prepared to stand with him in moments when anyone to whom the follower is con-

7. Matt 10:36.
8. Wink, *The Powers that Be*, 77.
9. Mark 3:35.
10. Mark 10:29–30.
11. Witherington, *Matthew*, 225.
12. Wink, *The Powers that Be*, 121.

nected chooses not to follow Christ. If following Christ will disrupt even the most humble and intimate human relationships (son against father, mother against daughter, etc.), it follows that loyalty to Christ will create disruption in the wider scope of relational existence, including the political. No dimension of life will go gently untouched by adherence to the way of Jesus. He was using one extreme to assert the full gamut of social patterns that would be affected by a commitment to follow him. Christ's followers must be prepared to be faithful to him, even when socio-economic, ethnic, and attachments of citizenship are at stake.

Christ came to proclaim the irrupting of God's reign. Prior to the fulfillment of God's reign, however, "even the peace Jesus bequeaths his disciples will have its setting in the midst of a hostile world."[13] Because the world is not of God, it will simply not allow the gospel a peaceful existence. Choosing to follow Christ will mean choosing not to follow the world, even while living in the world. A person who merely admires Christ will face no such decisions.

When culture, society, or other influences are allowed to moderate his claims Christ becomes someone merely to be admired. Such a Christ may offer peace but carry no sword. The peace offered by this reassuring Christ will make perfect sense to the world, affirming its self-defined status quo. If Christ brings no sword, the values of the world stand as testament to the world's own definitive wisdom. If Christ brings no sword, he makes no political claims. If Christ makes no political claims, the world is free to ignore the reign of God. While the world may prefer a sword-less Christ, it does so at its own peril.

An apolitical Jesus speaks only what the world is willing to hear. When the church worships an apolitical Jesus, it speaks a form of the truth that is merely comfortable for the world. While that form of truth contentedly confirms the world's status quo, the truth of the gospel in Christ challenges it.

13. Carson, "Matthew," 52.

When the church worships faithfully according to the reign of God in Christ, it commits a political act that the world will utterly refute. God's political claims seek no compromise with the world's partisan political configurations. All of the world's regimes may stand, but only for a season. God's reign alone will prevail. The church, as agent of God's reign in the world, must understand the political nature of Christ's claims. Only then will the church understand that apoliticality in its worship is not an option.

The Christ extolled by the gospel does come with a sword. This Christ also brings peace, though not as the world understands it. It is this Christ that the church worships when it worships faithfully. In faithful worship, the followers of Christ choose. They claim the reign of God in Christ over all other loyalties; no dimension of life is exempt. There are no dichotomies. All realms of creation and time are under the sovereignty of the triune God. The psalmist gives voice to the ultimate political claim: "The earth is the LORD's and all that is in it, the world and those who live in it."[14] The world wants to operate as though Christ brings no sword, while finding the notion of Christ's peace appealing. The world believes it is not necessary to make the choices for which Christ calls. Yet Christ's peace is unattainable without the choices called for by Christ's sword.

In worship, and in contradiction to the choices the world makes, the church gives assent to the political claims of God and thus transcends the world; "it testifies that the world is not its own."[15] It is unbearable for the world (and all its empires) to think it is not in control of its own destiny. The reason the world denies the claims of Christ is that those claims speak a truth the world prefers not to hear. The world would favor an apolitical Christ, whose message can be controlled, co-opted, or even countermanded. "Voices that tell uncomfortable truths usually get silenced."[16] So it

14. Ps 24:1.
15. Wannenwetsch, *Political Worship*, 127.
16. Wright, *For All God's Worth*, 43.

was the day Rome nailed Christ to a cross, and so it has been for the followers of Christ who have worshiped and lived faithfully since that day.

The church aims its political critique at no particular worldly regime; "it is directed against the totalization of political existence in general."[17] This totalization proposes that the world can succeed, be complete, and be at peace through partisan political operations of its own design—through its own settled arrangements. When politics operate apart from the worship of the triune God and God's kingdom-coming, they create a worldly cultish following of their own making. Like any other power absent the authority of God-ward worship, politics will inevitably become idolatrous. As one such idolatry, worldly politics will claim supreme authority, virtually always becoming coercive and oppressive.

Worldly political power might be well understood to have a spiritual, though not necessarily godly, essence. God's people have always encountered such forces. Throughout history, the world's entities, whether cultural, political, or economic, have exhibited a tangible spirituality that can be categorized as powers and principalities.[18] It is possible to make various similar categorizations for our own day, including political, economic, and social powers—even the influences of technology and media. While a direct connotation from Paul's writings to modern times may not be viable, it is certain that principalities and powers (what he calls "cosmic authorities") are in force as they "influence human events and structures. What we call the state, the economy, the media, ideology—these are their instruments."[19]

The politics of worldly affairs may be considered principalities and powers or, viewed instrumentally, as being used by principalities and powers. For purposes here, the distinction is nonessential. What is essential first is the recognition that Christ

17. Wannenwetsch, *Political Worship*, 127.

18. Wink, *The Powers that Be*, 24.

19. Yoder, *He Came Preaching Peace*, 114.

confronted and defeated the principalities and powers; Scripture is clear.[20] They have been "disarmed but not destroyed" and have come under "the supreme dominion of Christ by what he has done on the cross."[21] The church must, indeed, contend with the powers and principalities, and the chief standing ground is worship. Second, worldly politics, being expressions of or subject to principalities and powers, are rebelliously adverse to the politics of God's reign. Therefore, Christ's confrontation with and defeat of the principalities and powers establishes the politics of God's reign as transcendent and definitive. When the church worships faithfully, it takes a stand on all issues against all worldly principalities and powers.

It is folly for the church to engage in political practices of the principalities and powers. The church is reckless when it responds to abuses of power in the world by participating in the same kinds of power, political or otherwise. When the church appropriates the manners of the principalities and powers, it denies the cross and resurrection.

The church's resistance to worldly political intrigues by choosing the way of Christ may be perceived as weakness. Yet that which gives an appearance of weakness from the world's perspective ultimately allows God to reveal God's reign through the followers of Christ. Paul writes that God's "power is made perfect in weakness."[22] Faithful worship understands that weakness in the eyes of the world makes way for God to tabernacle among God's people,[23] a concept itself invested with liturgical significance.

Faithful worship causes the church to live God's reign and stand against the domination, oppression, and violence perpetrated against humankind and creation by the principalities and powers. In that sense, Christ's followers worship as an act of resistance.

20. Eph 1:20–22; Col 2:14–15; 1 Pet 3:22, etc.
21. Newbigin, *The Gospel in a Pluralist Society*, 204.
22. 2 Cor 12:9.
23. Dawn, *Powers, Weakness, and the Tabernacling of God*, 31.

Service to two masters is untenable according to Christ, and the sword he brings is the sword of choice—chose this day the one you will serve. Thus Christ's *ekklesia* must make its preference known: The kingdom of God or the principalities-and-powers-controlled kingdoms of this world?

CHRIST OR CAESAR? THE CHURCH MUST CHOOSE

This Messiah Jesus Christ made a number of daring claims. He declared that he came bringing a sword as a sign of peace, that he had power to free captives, that a person's allegiance to God transcended even the most intimate of relationships—the family, and that the least members of society were to be highly esteemed.

A charismatic teacher—especially one who claimed to be the Son of God—would have been closely watched by the Empire and its emperor. Attempts by imperial force and even by the religious leaders of the day to silence Jesus ultimately failed. After Jesus' resurrection and ascension, it became increasingly apparent that the movement involving his followers would not only survive but also flourish. The Empire would have to seek other means of neutralizing the upstart *ekklesia*.

The Constantinian solution involved imperial approval for the faith, as much to control it by merging it into Roman culture as anything else. By the time Christianity became the state religion, the church and the gospel it proclaimed were intertwined with imperial society. Thus began the centuries-long struggle to resist the enticements of empire, eventually involving the nation-states of the latter centuries followed by the proud new nation birthed in the thirteen colonies of America.

Worship is a political endeavor. The very statement always raises the essential question: Which or whose politics does the worship sanction? The church must choose its politics, and accurately express those politics in its worship. In light of the encounter of *ekklesia* with empire, the church is faced with three viable choices.

First, the church can choose to allow space within the body and the body's worship practice for the politics of Caesar. In this case, nationalism becomes a part of the church's creed; expressing a preference for the nation confuses or even diminishes Christians' sense of true citizenship in the reign of God. Under this paradigm, God's kingdom is coming, but is not in any tangible sense a present reality. Displays of nationalistic fervor are reinforced by the presence of symbols representing the nation. The nation's rituals and celebrations become part of the church's liturgical practice.

If, as argued above, the primary impulse of nationalism is self-preservation and the church's identity is partially shaped by the incorporation of nationalistic symbols and rituals, the church must accept the preservation of the state as part of its agenda along with the actions necessary to accomplish that preservation. History has proven that the nation-state will resort to coercion and violence in defense of itself; these are certainly antithetical to the teachings of Jesus. Under the influence of nationalistic self-protection, whatever peace the church enjoys will be provided by Caesar rather than by Christ and the sword that Jesus brings will be replaced by the one wielded by Caesar.

Under nationalism's sway, the nation's supporting practices—including social, economic, and partisan political operations—may be welcomed by the church. Consumerism, materialism, and market capitalism certainly combine for a healthy economic status. Each, however, entails practices that can become antithetical to the gospel. Consumerism, for example, easily translates into satisfaction through personal preference as opposed to honoring one another above self[24] and liquidating possessions to contribute to the needs of all in the body.[25] Materialism highlights acquisi-

24. Rom 12:10b.
25. Acts 2:45.

tion and gain more than sharing with others[26] and being willing to identify with the least of these.[27] Market capitalism can ignore the sometimes exploitive and demeaning conditions necessary for goods to be produced, moved, and marketed.

The practice of marketing, so necessary to these economic practices, is "embedded with a set of convictions, practices, and narratives" which are questionable in light of God's offer of grace in Christ.[28] The church unwittingly becomes one more niche and source of revenue for the economic engine that drives the empire and its agenda, domestic as well as foreign. The gospel even becomes marketable; the commodification of experience (observed, for example, in theme parks and many popular fast food restaurants) has encroached into the church's practice. Few if any dimensions of the church's communal worship experience have escaped treatment as a commodity in some form or mode. Worship as a commodity tends to diminish liturgy; "the authentic political character of the Christian community disintegrates as soon as the community is conceived under the category of audience."[29] The politics of Caesar tend to sell quite well, especially when combined with religion. The politics of God's reign are not quite as good for business, however, and tend to resist commodification.

To be sure, the market economy enjoyed largely throughout the U.S. provides the church in this country access to economic resources unparalleled in history, and the God-ward stewardship of these resources is a challenging task. Yet the residual effect of overt participation in such nationalistically acceptable activities may come at a high cost. The church's willing participation in such nationalistic endeavors is far too easily perceived as approval for whatever means the nation—in this case the U.S.—chooses to employ in order to sustain itself and extend its influence within its

26. Acts 2:44.
27. Matt 25:40.
28. Kenneson and Street, *Selling Out the Church*, 36.
29. Wannenwetsch, *Political Worship*, 25.

borders and across the globe. The full extent to which the practices mentioned immediately above can become oppressive and idolatrous has been well documented in other places. Suffice it to say here these nationalisms are arguably more of a deterrent to the church's faithfulness to the gospel than they are an encouragement.

The defused concept of religion, as noted above, has been instrumental in disenfranchising the church from its original identity. That has made it possible for nationalism to seek religious meaning. In so doing it either inserts itself into the church's practice, or competes with the church for adherence among its citizenry. Religion as an instrument of nationalistic fervor is hardly territory that the church needs to defend. It has become, in effect, a means of avoiding God, "an attempt to mitigate the demands of revelation upon" followers of Christ.[30] Such religion allows humanity to construct its own definitive narrative, albeit in terms and themes that may invoke God (or gods, or even no god at all). Nationalism is one among many of these narratives. Faithful worship, however, calls worshipers back to the narrative of God revealed in Christ, and thus transcends religious nationalism.

A crucial example of religious complicity with empire is recorded in John's gospel.[31] After having been questioned thoroughly by Pilate after his arrest, the Jews rebuffed Pilate's attempts to release Jesus having found him guiltless of breaking any law. They shouted, "Everyone who claims to be a king sets himself against the emperor." (Earlier, Jesus had claimed to have a kingdom that was not from this world, and refused to deny his kingship.[32]) Jesus was ultimately displayed publicly before the Jews. Pilate declared, "Here is your King!" to which they replied, "Away with him! Crucify him!" Seeking to clarify their demand, Pilate asked, "Shall I crucify your King?" The astounding response is credited to the chief priests: "We have no king but the emperor." Perhaps their

30. Cavanaugh, "God is Not Religious," 112.
31. John 19:1–16.
32. John 18:33–38.

unmet expectations got the best of the Jews whose earlier acclamations of welcome as Jesus arrived in Jerusalem were mere forgotten echoes. The politics of the emperor were preferable to the politics of a Messiah whose politics they could not control.

The second option available to the church regarding politics is to claim that it has no politics—that it has depoliticized itself. Depoliticization is an appealing option; disentangling the church from politics makes sense in a highly politicized and polarized nation such as the U.S. However, the church's record on attempts to step away from worldly politics is blemished at best. Its inability to resist the entanglements is a sign that it has abandoned the politics of the Messiah. The Enlightenment privatization of faith left politics to the public arena, a realm distinct from the private realm allowed to the church. Absent the church's distinct reign-of-God political deportment, politics have, throughout modern times, been defined and owned by national governments.

It is perilous, however, for the church to maintain that its worship has no politics. Indeed, a church with no political claims is not the true church since it allows a realm of existence into which it will not speak prophetically on behalf of its Sovereign. If the church believes that God is sovereign over all things yet refuses to engage some sphere of life, does it not decline to participate in God's sovereignty? If the church begs off God's sovereignty in any regard, can its worship be truly faithful?

If the church does not claim the politics of the reign of God in Christ accurately within its worship, the church will inevitably claim—or, more pointedly, will be claimed by—the politics of Caesar. Once so chosen, Caesar's intrigues will dictate the necessity for its demands to be honored by the church, though not exclusively. Caesar is just wise enough to know that the attempt of a complete overthrow of God in the church might just make the church of little or no value to the empire's agenda. A church with no God is of little use to Caesar. Caesar is fully content to share the platform with God in the church's worship.

Pluralism as practiced within democratic capitalism is well known to Caesar. The liturgical practice of the empty shrine is one Caesar would gladly extend into the church. Caesar would relish the opportunity of defining the nature of God for *ekklesia*. While Caesar is content with such arrangements, the triune God encountered in the story of ancient Israel and in the person of Jesus Christ is not likely to be so inclined.

The church at various times and places in its history has made faithful attempts at understanding and exhibiting a political ethic according to its interpretation of Jesus' life, ministry, and teachings. That stated, under the mantle of Christendom, the church functioned as though politics was primarily the province of governmental entities. Whatever politics the church did practice, more times than not, were styled after the partisan politics of whatever civil entity happened to prevail at any given time. The emergence of the modern nation-state solidified that configuration, effectively assigning control of the political realm of the world to the nation-state. Thus the church and its constituents either eschewed politics altogether or appropriated its host nation's politics as its own. Thus "Christians have continually been tempted to view politics as a necessary evil."[33]

This dichotomy has not only distracted the church from its correct political nature, it has neutered the church for the gospel by forcing it to practice politics according to the world's standards. The church cannot compete with the world on the world's terms politically; it was never intended to do so. Christians have rather looked to government as a means of accomplishing at least some of what the original *ekklesia* was called to be and do. This is particularly true in the U.S., where Christians "have come to depend on the nation, rather than the church, as their primary instrument of social change and communal influence."[34] The highly-touted separation of church and state may hold sway at some levels, yet is

33. Wannenwetsch, *Political Worship*, 175.
34. Webber and Clapp, *People of the Truth*, 6.

porous in practice since the partition of politics and religion (when religion is defined as distinct from Christ-following) is anything but absolute.

Under Christendom, the church developed a taste for worldly political operations. The church's first two options—choosing Caesar's politics, and choosing depoliticization (which is likely to lead back to the first) deny the church its role as the Jesus-called proclaimer of the reality of the reign of God. In order for the church to recapture the integrity of the gospel, the church must be effectively weaned from its dependence on practices grounded in the world's partisan structures. This depoliticization will only be effective if accompanied by an intentional reorientation to faithfulness in the politics of the reign of God.

The third option—the *repoliticization of worship*—is the definitive act in that reorientation. This is a demanding task, inevitably creating as much tension within the church itself as it does between the church and the world. Yet it is a necessary task.

The claim of political import for the things Jesus said and did during his earthly life has stirred vigorous discussion and even misunderstanding among his followers. In light of the well-established Enlightenment dichotomy described above—politics is secular and public, and religion is sacred and private—the notion that politics attends solely to worldly affairs is pervasive. However, not all congregations or faith communities accept this construct or attend to this issue in the same manner. Some have learned to perceive participation in partisan political affairs as a step outside of its own sphere, simply accepting their role in spiritual affairs and leaving the rest to the state. Others have readily stepped into partisan politics, ostensibly to represent the agenda of the gospel yet using statecraft to do so. This book has asserted that Jesus' life, ministry, and teachings were, indeed, political. It has also maintained that his politics are an accurate reflection of the reign of God, and that the politics of this reign are distinct from all worldly politics. In Jesus, it is possible to discover the reign of God.

More than a few sources suggest that various worldly political entities have incorporated into their structure principles consonant with the teachings of Jesus and the biblical tradition, and such arguments are generally sustainable. This is certainly true of the U.S. with its tenable reliance on moral principles (e.g. adherence to some of the Decalogue [prohibitions from killing, stealing, etc.] and "the encouragement of attitudes of forgiveness and generosity"[35]) from within the Judeo-Christian tradition. What must be noted here, however, is that God's covenantal relationship (first with ancient Israel and then with the Second Testament *ekklesia*-become-the-church) specifies that God's people have been called into existence for the express purpose of representing God in the world. Claims of an unusual prerogative to that role by any other entity—statist or otherwise—in any time or any place must be dismissed out of hand.

If the church expects its Christ-following to be faithful, it must take the assertions stated above and the attendant implications seriously. The exclusivity of God's covenantal mission for the church is likely to create anxiety, certainly on the part of worldly political entities but also within the church itself. That tension, however, is due to the irruption of God's reign into a history-encompassing world scene that in general exists at odds with that reign. The strain produced by this radical in-breaking is precisely part and parcel of the subversive and redemptive nature of the gospel. The church risks its faithfulness to God in Christ when it mitigates the radicality of its encounter with the world.

Jesus broke socio-political conventions by eating with prostitutes and other sinners, befriending tax collectors, asking a Samaritan woman for a drink of water, and telling stories about property owners with questionable scruples and priests who refused to help a battered stranger. He also paid deep attention to the people in society who were perceived to have—and be—the least. He championed the value of all persons whose life situations

35. Carter, *The Culture of Disbelief*, 87.

were made more desperate by fellow-citizens who used their own position to acts as lords over the needy rather than seeking to serve.[36] Jesus' politics were deeply integrated into an over-arching conceptualization of life and the world. It was not necessary for him to speak about such matters apart from other issues. As noted above, those who saw and heard Jesus were aware of the political messages he was sending. He did nothing to indicate such interpretations were misunderstandings.

It would have been relatively simple for Rome to deal with Jesus had he cast himself as a bold revolutionary like others before and after him. Jesus' political critique was subtle, however, and created an intense dilemma for Roman authorities. The nuances of the politics of Jesus make it possible to either underestimate the significance of his politics or over interpret them. This is just as true for Jesus' followers as it is for worldly political entities.

Luke records one of the more overt statements Jesus made regarding political issues.[37] The chief priests and elders were questioning Jesus' authority while Jesus was in Jerusalem. Dissatisfied with the outcome of their own inquiry, they sent spies[38] to attempt to trap Jesus so they could find reason to have him arrested. Their inquiry was not profound on its face, but it was provocative. "'Is it lawful for us to pay taxes to the emperor, or not?'"[39] Jesus asked for a coin of the realm, and in turn inquired of the assembly whose image was visible on it. Obviously, Caesar, the emperor, appeared there. Jesus said, "'Give to the emperor the things that are the emperor's, and to God the things that are God's.'"[40] The encounter

36. Matt 20:25; Mark 10:42; Luke 22:25.

37. Luke 20:20–26; also Matt 22:15–22; Mark 12:13–17.

38. Mark 12:13 notes they were Herodians and Pharisees.

39. Luke 20:22. The inquisitors betrayed their own treachery in near-laughable flattery by a comment preceding the question: "'Teacher, we know that you are right in what you say and teach, and you show deference to no one, but teach the way of God in accordance with truth.'" Luke 20:21.

40. Mark 12:17. Note in the NRSV Jesus simply refers to "the emperor," but not as Caesar or by name.

ends rather abruptly since, "they were not able in the presence of the people to trap him by what he said; and being amazed by his answer, they became silent."

On one level, Jesus was making a simple point about what was right. It was obvious that the spies had the coin with them. Jesus asked them to produce it, and they did so. The use of a coin implied that the user was drawing on the value of that coin for the necessities of life. People who earned a wage had access to the value of the coin and, therefore, participated in the commerce of Roman society. The worth of that coin was guaranteed by the person whose image it bore; "people who benefit from Caesar must pay him for it."[41] In his first epistle, Peter speaks affirmatively regarding this issue, noting that by doing what is right in regard to human institutions those who are foolish will be silenced—just as the spies were after Jesus' response.[42]

While Jesus was not making a singular definitive statement regarding any relationship between the empire and God's reign, this is "Jesus' only saying directly relating to affairs of state."[43] He was also not establishing a realm for the emperor (or empire) separate from God's sovereignty. God's claims of rule over all creation and all that dwell on the earth would have been well known by those who heard his words. If anything, Jesus was relegating the emperor's influence to trivial status.[44] In his commentary of this event, Cyril of Alexander states that "God does not require of [his

---

41. Marshall, "Luke," 1012.

42. 1 Pet 2:13–17.

43. Bock, *Baker Exegetical Commentary*, 1613.

44. "[Jesus] has not escaped the issue, however, by dividing the world into two spheres, one belonging to the emperor and the other to God. Such dichotomous thinking would be entirely alien to ancient anthropology. Instead, while not denying the possibility of obedience to Caesar, Jesus asserts the prior and more fundamental claim of God on all human beings, on human existence itself." Green, "The Gospel of Luke," 715.

followers] anything corruptible and temporary,"[45] implying that such descriptors were apt for the empire and the emperor's rule.

These Herodians and Pharisees asked a question that, on its face, required a response of preference for one or the other. For Jesus to choose Caesar over God would have pleased the inquisitors by allowing the high priests to degrade Jesus' influence with the people. It would have weakened all of Jesus' other teachings that encouraged those who were marginalized by Roman society. If Jesus had denied any form of payment to Caesar, the inquisitors would have been equally pleased since they could have turned Jesus over to their Roman masters as an insurrectionist. The tribute required by Rome was burdensome to the common people and served as a harsh reminder of their subjugation; a refusal to pay was treasonable and hence punishable. Either way, the trap would have been a victory.

It is unlikely that Jesus was concerned that something would be offered to God that was Caesar's. Jesus knew the temptation, rather, would be to offer to Caesar something that by right belonged to God. By responding the way he did, Jesus revealed the complicity in the hearts of the interrogators about ultimate allegiance. "Serving as Rome's tribute-gatherer and comporting itself so as to win public favor . . . the Jerusalem leadership appears to have sided with the Empire, against the purpose and rule of God."[46]

The intrigue of the Herodians and Pharisees at the behest of the high priests was remarkable. They devised "a question designed to force Jesus to make a choice between Rome and Israel."[47] Their ruse did not fool Jesus, and he altered the tenor of the question with his response. Allegiance to any worldly entity or leader is not synonymous with allegiance to God.

At no time, in this instance or any other, does Jesus deny the right of the state to exist, even a repressive one like Rome. "[T]he

45. Cyril of Alexandria, *Commentary on the Gospel of St. Luke*, 539.

46. Ibid., 715.

47. Bock, *Baker Exegetical Commentary*, 1614.

character of a state is not grounds for challenging the state's right to organize itself at the political and social levels."[48] His calm encouragement to pay what Caesar requires is echoed later in Paul's missive to the followers of Christ in Rome, who writes, "Pay to all what is due to them—taxes to whom taxes are due . . ."[49] What is clear is that the presence of any government, authorities whose existence has been established by God, must not be confused with the reign of God. It is also important to avoid misunderstanding the distinction between worldly political entities and the covenantal existence and responsibilities of the people of God as alternative *polis*.

While acting in a provocative manner in relation to the Roman Empire, the church still valued the existence of the Empire. It had a certain function, namely to preserve stability in the present age for the purposes of the gospel. In fact, the structure of Roman society itself was a servant of God for "encouraging the good and restraining evil, i.e., to serve peace, to preserve the social cohesion in which the leaven of the gospel [could] build the church."[50] The apostle Paul affirms this very concept in his letter to the *ekklesia* at Rome by writing that "governing authorities" are "God's servant for your good."[51] This hardly draws Rome to center stage in God's cosmic narrative, yet neither does it deny Rome a role in the story.

Inevitably, the loyalty expected by empire will conflict with the allegiance required by God. Persons who choose to follow Christ will face a decision. God makes claims, and so does Caesar. The empire, however insistent it may be in asserting its authority, ultimately "finds its appropriate function within and subservient

---

48. Ibid., 1613.
49. Rom 13:1–7.
50. Yoder, *The Original Revolution*, 72–23.
51. Rom 13:1, 4.

to God's universal dominion."[52] God's claims always trump the claims of imperial sovereignty.

Admittedly, the repoliticization of worship is a concept that is easily misunderstood and requires a peculiar frame of reference. Any construct that considers politics strictly the purview of the world assures an abuse of the church, the gospel, and the church's worship. Since the church has existed for such a lengthy time under this very misconception, it is necessary to first depoliticize worship; in other words, to disorient—or even detoxify—the church's worship away from any inclination toward partisan politics as practiced by worldly entities. Such a depoliticization of worship must not be allowed to stand as an end, however. Apoliticality only invites a relapse that may result in an even greater inclination toward the world's political scenarios in the worship life of the church.

Repoliticizing worship among followers of Christ in the U.S. (or in any nation for that matter) will never be easy. Yet the repoliticization of Christian worship is crucial, for it can hasten the church's renewed practice of the transcendent politics of the reign of God. This will only happen as the church explores its nature as alternative *polis* and as it attends to Jesus Christ as the prototype of God's total sovereignty over all of life and creation.

The confirmation of the church's repoliticized worship will be *the repoliticization of worshipers*. As these repoliticized Christ-followers worship faithfully, the reign of God in Christ will be revealed in their midst and through their provocative presence in but not of the world. To worship faithfully in this manner will be to do so in anticipation of the fulfillment of *missio Dei* and the consummation of the eternal reign of God.

52. Green, "The Gospel of Luke," 715.

6

Glimpses of Worship in Kingdom Now, Kingdom Come

THE GRAND liturgy of the kingdom of heaven is to love God with the totality of heart, soul, mind, and strength and to love neighbor as self. This is the seed-bed from which faithful worship in the kingdom of God rises—two commandments inextricably bound denoting the breadth and depth of faithfulness in worship. The first and greatest commandment is the context for living out the second. Honoring the second would certainly be good, yet if disjoined from the first it would be deficient of kingdom significance. Yet fulfilling the first would be unfinished business without engaging in the second. Compelled by Christ's clarification of the two greatest commandments, all of the practices of loving the LORD God and neighbor are integrated as the work of the people of God—worship whole, and worship fulfilled.

The practices of faithful worship noted earlier—that such worship is specific, exclusive, Christological, cosmic, and eschatological—are most vividly and accurately expressed within the context of God's kingdom. The specific use of the word kingdom in the gospels and other terms like it throughout Scripture implies a communal reality born of the will and sovereignty of triune God. It is a unique and holy kingdom unlike any worldly empire, already present in Christ and expressed through Christ's body, the church. God's Spirit is at work in time and space setting the stage for Christ's second advent, at which time the fullness of God's reign will be revealed in a new heaven and earth.

God's intention to create a people for Godself is pervasive in Scripture. "I will make of you a great nation," God said to Abram, "and I will bless you, and make your name great, so that you will be a blessing."[1] The balance of the first Testament describes the history of that nation as it encounters other nations of the earth. The records of the lives and words of judges, kings, and prophets tell a story that is replete with sagas of sinfulness and redemption, defeat and renewal, exile and return. These people were called into covenant with the God of Abraham, Isaac, and Jacob. At the heart of the covenant was worship, "the presentation and address of all of life to this single loyalty, to the God who summons, forms, rescues, and commands Israel."[2] Ultimately, the covenant required exclusivity; true worship was reserved for God alone. Their syncretistic attachment to the values, rituals, and gods of other nations provided the momentum for ancient Israel's constant pendulum-swing from worship to idolatry and back.

God makes God's presence known in the world in a way that captures the attention of the nations. Yet the nations persist in acting as though God plays little or no part in their existence. In fact, in more than a few times and places, the nations have acted antagonistically toward the ways of the holy triune God. Consider the words of the psalmist:

> "Why do the nations conspire,
>   and the peoples plot in vain?
> The kings of the earth set themselves,
>   and the rulers take counsel together,
>   against the LORD and his anointed . . ."[3]

This premise is also pervasive throughout the whole of Scripture. People organize themselves into nations and empires,

1. Gen 12:2
2. Brueggemann, *Worship in Ancient Israel*, 7.
3. Ps 2:1–2.

claim rulers and kings for themselves, and make plans for success and life and safety. In service to their own nationalistic agendas, they plot against God, God's people, and God's Anointed One, Jesus.

Against the backdrop of the dialectic of these two persistent themes, Scripture highlights distinctives of what it means to be God's covenant people with a variety of provocative descriptions. All of them are necessary and none is sufficient alone to be comprehensive. This is particularly true of descriptors with provenance in both Testaments. Peter brings just such denotations to the fore by reminding his readers that they are "a chosen race, a royal priesthood, a holy nation . . . ."[4] The author draws on the words of God through Moses to the Israelites just prior to the consecration of the people and speaking the Law into existence. God's nation-creating claims on Israel are clear: "you shall be my treasured possession out of all the peoples . . . you shall be for me a priestly kingdom and a holy nation."[5]

In addition, the new creation in Christ brings about a re-ordering of relationships for the community of Christ's followers. Aliens and strangers become a new people, the household of God signals the new just economy of God's kingdom, and a new heaven and a new earth become home for God and God's chosen people. All of these images make it clear that the church is a political reality distinct from (not of) the world, yet existing in the world until the fullness of the reign of God in Christ is revealed. It is not separate from the world completely. Neither is it merely a "spiritual form of an already existing body."[6]

Before coming to Christ, Gentiles were "aliens from the commonwealth of Israel."[7] In Christ, however, the ethnic boundary ("dividing wall") was broken down, "that he might create in

4. 1 Pet 2:9.
5. Exod 19:5b–6a.
6. Harvey, *Another City*, 15.
7. Eph 2:11–12.

himself one new humanity in place of the two, thus making peace, and might reconcile both groups to God in one body . . . ."[8] Now, "you are no longer strangers and aliens, but you are citizens" writes Paul.[9] A new citizenship is conferred upon Christ's followers who thus become foreigners; they are no longer "nationals" in the worldly kingdom where they reside.[10] As participants in *ekklesia*— the alternative *polis*—those who follow Christ become aliens and strangers in the world, yet are now citizens in the reign of God.

The claim that Jews and Gentiles hold a common citizenship in Christ reinforces the political implications of *ekklesia*. The exclusivity of worshiping God in Christ proposes a profound inclusivity for all who choose to follow Jesus. Distinctions such as Jew and Greek, circumcised and uncircumcised, barbarian and Scythian, male and female, slave and free have no place in *ekklesia*.[11] None are aliens, none are strangers, all are elevated to the status of full citizens. Collectively, Christ's followers become "a chosen race . . . God's own people."[12] As alternative *polis* the church transcends all social configurations that trade on the artificiality of worldly distinctions.

The kinds of divisions noted above were well-ingrained in the society within which the first Christ-followers were being formed into the body of Christ. The struggle over these distinctions of

8. Eph 2:14–16.

9. Eph 2:19.

10. Wannenwetsch, *Political Worship*, 141. The author further notes: "Christians evidently saw themselves as a separate civil community within local life in the civil polity of the empire, even if they were not recognized as such by the state. This is emphatically documented in a testimony dating from the second century, the Epistle to Diognetus: 'Yet while living in Greek and barbarian cities . . . and following the local customs both in clothing and food and in the rest of life, they shew forth the wonderful and confessedly strange character of the constitution of their own citizenship. They dwell in their own fatherlands, but as if sojourners in them; they share all things as citizens, and suffer all things as strangers.' (5.4f.; trans. Kirsopp Lake)."

11. Gal 3:28 and Col 3:11.

12. 1 Pet 2:9.

ethnicity, socio-economic status, and gender bias was culturally-based with layers upon layers of unwritten boundaries. The re-orientation of these relationships under the unity of Christ's Spirit was an enormous task, requiring personal as well as communal courage. In this regard, the challenges faced by the church are as just as prevalent in the twenty-first century. The witness of the first century church through this re-ordering of relationships is just as important in our own day as it was then.

While Christ is insistently transcending and even dismantling such barriers, the world—and even the church under the influence of the world—is quite busy restacking the blocks, fashioning ever-more challenging obstacles that trade on ages-old biases. Labeling and dividing people into distinct groups are practices that make perfect sense to the world, which is precisely the reason the church should be wary of such strategies. If, in its gathering for worship (or any other purpose for that matter) the church practices the world's ways of categorizing and separating people, how then is the church different from the world? One of the essential paradoxes of Christ's gospel is that the influence of the church's communal witness is most effectual at points where the gospel runs counter to the world's manner of treating people. The church's witness hinges on its ability to behave in ways that the world simply does not understand and may even reject.

It is likely that the readers of Peter's epistle were Christians of both Gentile and Jewish background. Peter supports the Pauline concept of both having come together as a new race and having taken on a new identity as a nation; they are now the people of God. This new citizenship requires that distinctions of national origin as well as those of ethnic heritage be laid aside. Such a stipulation held great significance for two groups of people who had lived in relative antagonism. It is generally accepted that the Peter who authored the epistles bearing that name in the cannon of Scripture was among the twelve apostles who joined Jesus Christ in his earthly ministry. In that light this declaration in Peter's epistle may reflect the encounter of Jesus with the Herodians and Pharisees regarding the paying of taxes,[13] and Jesus' response when pressed to choose between Caesar and God. Peter's letter reminded his readers that they had been chosen by God and thereby stepped from one citizenship into a new one in the community of Christ-followers representing God's kingdom.

Paul also notes that followers of Christ become a part of the "household of God."[14] The Greek term *oikeios*[15] is a term that describes the living relationships that are "aimed at the survival of human beings in society."[16] It can refer to the more private family orientation of relationships in Christ in contrast to the more public image of citizenship in *ekklesia*. Yet it is essential for a biblical ecclesiology since the fullness and radicality of God's reign draw momentum from the complimentary interplay of citizenship and household.

In regard to ultimate residency, Paul reminds readers that "our citizenship is in heaven, and it is from there that we are expecting a Savior, the Lord Jesus Christ."[17] The writer of Hebrews also makes it clear that God's people have no city here in the current world, but look instead "for the city that is to come."[18] Among the vibrant images in Revelation is an identification of just such a city. "And I saw the holy city," writes John, "the new Jerusalem, coming down out of heaven from God . . ."[19] Jerusalem had a unique and holy place within Israel's conception of itself as God's people. Yet

13. Matt 22:15–22; Luke 20:20–26; Mark 12:13–17.

14. Eph 2:19.

15. Appearing as οἰκεῖος in Scripture referring to one's family, domestic, and intimate relationships.

16. Meeks, *God the Economist*, 33.

17. Phil 3:20.

18. Heb 13:14.

19. Rev 21:2.

John's account describes a new city designed for the new people of God—all "those who conquer" in Christ.[20]

As noted above, the Greek word *leitourgia*[21] provides necessary footing for a full understanding of the broader implications of worship. It appears in the New Testament as but one of the worship-related terms used in the Greek text—it appears a mere six times—and it is the New Testament term for worship most widely used throughout the history of the church. *Leitourgia* is typically translated as *service*, and has come to mean the work of the people of God. It is also distinctly communal in context and expression. Although liturgy may entail specific acts by individuals, its primary connotation involves practices engaged in within the communal setting for the benefit of whole community.

Certainly, the church should recognize that its presence in the world is a witness to God's activity in the world. The church that is focused on *missio Dei* understands "that its most credible form of witness (and the most 'effective' thing it can do for the world) is the actual creation of a living, breathing, visible community of faith."[22] In light of the second Testament's claims of an alternative citizenship for Christ's followers, *ekklesia's* presence in the world is provocative. Its encounter with empire, that would dispute such claims, requires a strength that can only be experienced in community. Such a community must have "the social strength to incarnate values that are antagonistic at key points to the world around [it]."[23]

Note again Peter's use of the identifier *royal priesthood* in conjunction with his description of Christ's followers as a *holy na-*

20. Rev 21:7.

21. The terms λειτουργίᾳ and λειτουργίας are used by Luke, Paul, and the author of Hebrews. The original meaning refers to service done by someone who holds a religious or civic office, having influence on the common life of the community. It could also mean priestly or Levitical service. Yet another connotation in the second Testament is *the liturgy of life*.

22. Hauerwas and Willimon, *Resident Aliens*, 47.

23. Snyder, *Liberating the Church*, 115.

tion. The pairing of adjectives to nouns here is noteworthy. Under less inspired hands, *royal nation* and *holy priesthood* might have made more sense. Yet in Peter and Exodus, the significance is compounded by interweaving the meanings, thus investing both with liturgical and political meaning. In this statement Peter creates an organic whole, linking the responsibilities of priesthood and citizenship in Christ. The liturgical and political are fully integrated into a seamless whole.

The role of priests in Israel's liturgical practices was to represent God to the people and the people to God. The distinction in Christ, however, is that all are priests—all are responsible for worship and for calling others to do the same. This is faithful worship, and is the most accurate witness the church can give regarding the kingdom of heaven: service to God who alone is worthy of worship, service to the body of Christ itself, and service to the world in which the church exists as Christ's representative in and across time.

In yet another evocative image, the triune nature of Godself strengthens the church's identity as an entirely counter-cultural community. The "subtle explanation of the divine oneness"[24] of the Father, Son, and Holy Spirit known as *perichoresis* acknowledges that the members of the Trinity co-inhere in regard to the creative, redemptive, and re-creative endeavors of God. Based on its identification with the triune God, the church orders itself within "an ecclesiology of *perichoresis*."[25] The relationships within *perichoretic* ecclesiology transcend all cultural, societal, socio-economic, gender, and ethnic boundaries. Given the communal pattern of the Trinity, the *koinonia* of the church becomes a reflection of the trinitarian character of God. Relationships exhibiting selfless love, persistent mutuality, purposeful coexistence, and vibrant single-mindedness testify to the unmistakable imprint of God's character in and through the lives of God's people. Worship within *ekklesia* that lives the reality defined by trinitarian wholeness offers a mark-

24. Butin, *The Trinity*, 35.
25. Gunton, *The Promise of Trinitarian Theology*, 78.

edly distinct witness that surpasses temporal hopes of the world's various expressions of community.

Christ, being the kingdom in himself, redeems people into himself and thus into God's kingdom. Christ's followers henceforth become active participants in all manner of kingdom endeavors. As kingdom people Christ's followers are drawn by Holy Spirit into transformational practices that signal the redemption of all things in the created order.[26] The fact that in Christ all social statuses are transcended and re-ordered is just the tip of the redemptive iceberg. The coming of the reign of God in Christ will result in a return to *shalom*. This is no mere peace brought on by a cessation of chaos and clatter, however. In the fullest biblical sense, "shalom means *universal flourishing, wholeness, and delight* – a rich state of affairs in which natural needs are satisfied and natural gifts fruitfully employed, a state of affairs that inspires joyful wonder as its Creator and Savior opens doors and welcomes the creatures in

---

26. Cavanaugh proposes that one dimension of salvation is that it "is essentially a matter of making peace among competing individuals." This is valuable in contrasting the Enlightenment's "essential individualism of the state" with "the created unity of the human race found in the Christian interpretation of Genesis 1–2." He contends, as a result, that "[i]t is in soteriology . . . that the ends of the Christian *mythos* and the state *mythos* seem to coincide." The distinction is important in light of a strong claim for a biblical counter-politicality against the rights of individuals tendered by the Enlightenment and statist agendas that divide groups of people based on differentiating characteristics. Cavanaugh, *Theopolitical Imagination*, 18–19.

Fiorenza notes this expansive understanding of redemption as well. "Christian theology . . . has been criticized for understanding redemption primarily as spiritual or as related to the invisible realm of human souls without reference to the external world. If redemption were so understood, it would be limited to spiritual life, and religion would have the function mainly of saving souls by bringing them into a spiritual community with God and Christ. I do not intend to discuss this spiritualistic and individualistic understanding of redemption, but rather to demonstrate that the author of Rev., John, did not share this view. Instead, he conceives of redemption and salvation in political terms and in socio-economic categories. John asserts that redemption involves liberation from bondage and slavery and that salvation gives new dignity to those who have been redeemed through the death of Jesus Christ." Fiorenza, *Revelation*, 68.

whom he delights."[27] The glory of God will be made manifest as all creation will join the full force of their renewed perfection in praise to the Redeemer-Creator. In contrast to the ultimate failure of all the world's settled arrangements to bring true reconciliation, the triune God will bring all things under Christ's feet with the eternal warranty of wholeness where there has been division, flourishing where there has been death, and delight where there has been distress. The worship of all false gods will be roundly and finally diminished to the perpetual point of no return.

The Revelation of John is a message of just such cosmic restoration. Its intricacies and dynamic images have intrigued and puzzled Christians and non-Christians of every persuasion across a wide theological spectrum. Among the many things that can be stated with certainty is that it is a magnificent call to worship that requires the attention of all people in all places in all times. The vibrant scenes and declarative texts weighted with worship by those claiming the name of Christ and the heavenly hosts are too numerous to examine here. Yet the understanding of the proposals above would be incomplete without drawing on Revelation's treasures for corroboration.

John, the author, found himself living in a first century season that bears some resemblance to this early part of the twenty-first century, even for the church in the U.S. Devotion to God in Christ had been trivialized, and the church was facing discrimination for its faithfulness. Caesar was claiming divine status, and it was a tempting claim for acceptance by the whole society. "Emperor worship, a feast to the senses that also guaranteed certain worldly security, was far more impressive than the Christian belief in an invisible God and crucified Savior that put its followers in danger of their lives."[28]

---

27. Plantinga, *Not the Way It's Supposed to Be*, 10.

28. Peterson, *Subversive Spirituality*, 87.

"Let anyone who has an ear listen to what the Spirit is saying to the churches."[29] This recurring litany appears toward the end of each of the letters to the seven churches in Revelation. It is not an unfamiliar refrain in Scripture, and its earlier forms[30] bring a particular force regarding worship to these letters and the Revelation itself.

The psalmist minces no words when characterizing idols: they are "the work of human hands. They have mouths, but do not speak; eyes, but do not see . . . ears, but do not hear; noses, but do not smell . . . hands, but do not feel; feet but do not walk; they make no sound in their throats."[31] Attention then turns to idolaters: "Those who make [idols] are like them; so are all who trust in them."[32] While idols have physical ears, eyes, mouths, etc., they have no life in them—they are completely without spiritual, intellectual, or emotional existence. The direct implication is that idolaters also have physical eyes and ears, yet they, too, lack life— they cannot see and hear, or respond to what the Spirit is saying

29. Rev 2:7, 11, 17, 29; 3:6, 13, 22.

30. Isaiah responds affirmatively to God's call: "Whom shall I send, and who will go for us?" It is followed by these instructions from God: "Go and say to this people: Keep listening, but do not comprehend; keep looking, but do not understand. Make the mind of this people dull, and stop their ears, and shut their eyes, so that they may not look with their eyes and listen with their ears, and comprehend with their minds, and turn and be healed." The language used by God is stunning, yet it is not Isaiah's actions or words that are creating deafness and blindness in these people. It is the idolatry of the people themselves that bears its harsh fruit in their lives. Isaiah 6:8–10.

Jesus' use of this passage from Isaiah is recorded in Mark 4:11–12 in speaking with his disciples and in John 12:37–41 as commentary on the unbelief of many people. Acts 28:17–28 records Paul's meeting with Jewish leaders in Rome; their contentiousness prompts him to affirm the Holy Spirit's words through Isaiah, identifying these Jews as persons whose dull hearts, sightless eyes, and deaf ears prevent them from understanding. It is also worth noting that Paul makes it clear that Israel's continued rejection of Jesus' Messiah-ship and the kingdom of God means the salvation of God would be proclaimed to Gentiles.

31. Ps 115:3–7 (verses 4–8 also appear in Ps 135:15–18).

32. Ps 115:8.

to the churches. The Spirit is speaking to those who have been counted among the faithful, but whose hearts and minds may have been dulled by idolatry.

Further, the communal nature of Revelation's message aims its critique of idols and idolatry not merely at the seven churches, but to all empires and nations as well. Only the worship of the one true God will suffice. Idolatry is forbidden and brings ruin.

In Revelation, all empires in all times and all places are called to account. The record of John's vision clearly counters the claims of Rome, and in so doing Rome "was linked typologically to all kingdoms and empires (cf. Rev. 17–18)."[33] Empires are not alone in rebuke, however. The congregations identified in the first three chapters also fall under this stringent critique. Revelation "recognizes that there is a false religion not only in the blatant idolatries of power and prosperity, but also in the constant danger that true religion falsify itself in compromise with such idolatries and betrayal of the truth of God."[34]

The clarity of the voices heard throughout the scenes envisioned by John call all creation to attention in anticipation of the Eschaton. The specificity of the faithful in proclaiming their loyalty and worship to God and to the Lamb is stunning. The display of the political reordering of heaven and earth is equally astonishing. By offering all glory and praise and honor and blessing to God and to the Lamb, worshipers are affirming the politics of God's reign in Christ. It all hinges on the clarity of the worshiping multitude. "What is surprising in Revelation is not that worship was political, but that worship of the One on the throne *excluded* worship of other gods or deified emperors."[35] The followers of Christ in our own day dare not do less.

As noted above, the first gathering of Christ-followers began to use terms to describe itself (*ekklesia*) and its message (gospel)

33. Harvey, *Another City*, 19.
34. Bauckham, *The Theology of the Book of Revelation*, 162.
35. Howard-Brook and Gwyther, *Unveiling Empire*, 206.

that were in the political vocabulary of Roman and Greek society. This was not merely coincidence, nor was it a matter of convenience. The early Christ-followers were making it clear that they believed the reign of God announced by Christ represented a political entity the stature of which was no less than that of Rome. At issue for this first-century movement identified with Christ was "Who was qualified to rule over empire? Was it the god Caesar or the God of Jesus?"[36] By using the same language as the Romans to announce that the reign of God was at hand, Christ's followers were serving notice on Rome (and, by extension, all worldly empires). When two persons or entities claim sovereignty, one must yield at the end of the day. Rome's hegemony was at stake.

John's account of the Revelation takes that use of language to its fullest degree. The first members of *ekklesia* claimed that Jesus was Lord and in so doing denied that status to Caesar. In Revelation, John claims that empire now belongs to Jesus and his followers.

> [Y]ou have made them to be a kingdom
> and priests serving our God,
> and they will reign on earth.
> The kingdom of the world has become
> the kingdom of our Lord
> and of his Messiah,
> and he will reign forever and ever.
> Now have come the salvation and the power
> and the kingdom of our God
> and the authority of his Messiah . . .[37]

The claim that denied lordship to Caesar is followed a second claim, denying *imperium* to Rome. Rome's version of its myth (myth being "symbolic communication within a given cultural and political system"[38]) was built around its use of the word *imperium*. Traditionally translated as "kingdom" or "reign" in the first-centu-

36. Ibid., 225.
37. Rev 5:10, 11:15, and 12:10 respectively.
38. Ibid., 113.

ry world of the early Christ-followers, the use of the term had one primary meaning: the Roman Empire. The use of that term was intended to symbolize to the known world that Rome's culture and politics defined life for all persons. Rome was not just one *imperium* among others—it was *the* Empire. Denying Rome its self-claimed due was an incitement of the highest order. "Most interpretations of the 'kingdom of God' fail to appreciate the depth of this mythic challenge to imperial power. They either privatize the challenge (i.e., the 'kingdom of God' is inside the human heart), or place it outside the realm of human action (e.g., after death, after the end of the world). Both these tracks fail to capture the radical character of John's vision of empire that turns the world upside down."[39]

The use of the terms "kingdom" and "priests" in Revelation 5:10 "designate the bearers of political power and sacral authority."[40] This concept was not wholly unique to the Revelation, and it signals the close relationship between religion and politics in antiquity. As in other instances highlighted above, terms referring to similar expressions in the broader culture are constantly invested with new meanings related to God's kingdom. This imprimatur of God's presence signals the full extent to which God's kingdom will infiltrate all relationships in the new heaven and new earth. The overt themes of worship in the Revelation make it clear that God, by establishing God's reign over and against Rome's Empire (with Rome being typological for all empires), calls for persons to decide: "one must choose whether one falls down in joyous worship or in stubborn resistance to . . . God."[41]

Given the context of this vigorous confrontation of empire in Revelation, one further point of vigilance is necessary. As the church takes seriously its participation in the in-breaking of God's reign, discernment must be exercised in order to resist the temptations of worldly power and influence. "The essential form of Christian

39. Howard-Brook and Gwyther, *Unveiling Empire*, 225.
40. Fiorenza, *Revelation*, 68.
41. Howard-Brook and Gwyther, *Unveiling Empire*, 207.

witness, which cannot be replaced by any other, is consistent loyalty to God's kingdom."[42] By refuting worldly power through this witness, characterized by the seemingly powerlessness of Jesus, the church can claim truth and defeat the lies of empire. The truth is that the world, if it is to come into the reign of God, must do so on God's terms, not its own terms. The church worships God, who is Spirit, by attending to God in spirit and truth.[43]

Revelation also acknowledges the extent of creation-wide worship. The catalogue of those giving voice in worship to God and to the Lamb begin with the "four living creatures," the "twenty four elders," the "many angels," and the "living creatures" counted as "myriads of myriads and thousands of thousands."[44] They are joined by the "great multitude that no one could count, from every nation, from all tribes and peoples and languages, standing before the throne and before the Lamb, robed in white, with palm branches in their hands."[45] Note here the tangible unity in this great gathered throng from across the ages and populations. The distinctions of ethnicity, nationality, and languages are acknowledged. Yet at the heart of this prophetic moment of eternal worship is the witness of the gospel transcending all worldly political constraints.

Passages such as these bring to the fore the intensity and intentionality of worship. They are also reminders to those who claim the name of Christ and worship God to safeguard themselves from idolatry. "It is only a purified vision of the transcendence of God that can effectively resist the human tendency to idolatry which consists in absolutizing aspects of this world."[46] Empire's impulse for self-preservation is, in effect, an attempt at absolutizing itself. Such attempts will not forestall the coming of the reign of God.

---

42. Bauckham, *The Theology of the Book of Revelation*, 163.
43. John 4:23.
44. Rev 4:8, 5:8, and 5:11.
45. Rev. 7:9.
46. Bauckham, *The Theology of the Book of Revelation*, 160.

Faithful worship will always reject all other gods in whatever guise they reveal themselves.

The provocative character of the Christian message is dependent upon one thing: the particularity of worship by those claiming to belong to God in Christ. America's pluralism carries the echoes of Rome's polytheistic culture since the U.S. Constitution allows persons—collectively or individually—to select God, or gods, or no god at all according to the dictates of conscience. No doubt those very freedoms will bring the message of God's kingdom into conflict with all other competing narratives. However, that has always been so. The biblical record from early in Genesis through the Revelation gives clear evidence of the persistent resistance by the ways and means of the world to the ways and means of God's kingdom. It is essential that the followers of Christ in every time and place worship faithfully in order to proclaim its witness to God in Christ faithfully.

In the summary portion of the Revelation, John identifies himself as the one who had experienced all the things contained therein. John fell down in awe at the feet of the angel who had shown it to him. "'You must not do that!'" the angel chided John, then making the angel's status as a fellow-servant with John very clear. The angel then speaks what may arguably be the point of the whole of scripture: "'Worship God!'"[47] God's reign in Christ by Holy Spirit represents a reality that will transcend and subsume all that the world perceives to be the ultimate reality. Worship that practices the reign of God acknowledges this truth not merely as a hope for the future, but by its faithfulness to all these things in the present.

47. Rev 22:8–9.

Epilogue

ORSHIP IS the way in which the church chooses. The communal gathering for worship is the occasion where *ekklesia* chooses. According to Scripture the choice is rather simple, though not always easy: worship the one true holy God, or worship in idolatry. To the extent that worship is a communal activity in which the church gathers for reminding itself of its commitments, worship becomes central to forming and sustaining the community. This on-going community-building process has rarely been attempted in a vacuum. The church has constantly lived within the dynamic tension between the kingdom of its Sovereign and a long history of worldly empires few of which have lasted more than a long season. More times than not, these worldly environments have been antagonistic to the notion of God as triune and to the expectations of the triune God for people and the whole of creation.

From its inception, the church's quandary regarding its surroundings has not abated. The book of Acts is replete with stories of the encounters between the *ekklesia* and the society within which it existed. The continuation of these interchanges is a thread woven throughout the history of the church. Many of these transactions reveal the pendulum swing of the church's attempts to live out the claims of Christ as valid while avoiding the entrapments of the world. The search for a viable praxis has been the topic of many writers and volumes of materials.

The worship of Christ by his earliest followers was not expressed in the context of a religionless society. If anything, during the days of Jesus' earthly life as well as in the years that followed his ascension, *ekklesia* existed within an exceedingly religious culture that not only encouraged the practice of multiple paganisms, but allowed for pluralistic religious diversity. Since Rome's imperial identity was so strongly invested with pagan and even caesaro-cultish religiosity, it was imperative that worship among Christ-followers be cast in distinctly different tones. So, too, the church's worship in our own day since worldly politics in every season of history so readily manifests its own brand of pious zeal.

By proclaiming the coming reign of God, Jesus was serving notice to the world that it was not in control of its own destiny nor of the ultimate meaning of its history. The seismic shift represented by the incarnation of God in Christ made it possible for those who would choose to follow Christ to see what may be all but invisible to the world regarding itself. As a result and over time, the earliest Christians embraced the fullness of the reign of God in Christ as ultimate reality.

Yet history and the world's inadequate attempts at stability, order, and peace are valuable. They are temporal space and time within which the progression of the coming of God's reign is accomplished. The culmination of the grand master narrative of God's redeeming adventure, focused in Christ and empowered by the Spirit, was noted above from the Revelation to John. To wit: "God's ultimate desire is to create from all nations a reconciled people living within a renewed creation and enjoying the presence of the triune God. This biblical vision of 'community' is the goal of history."[1]

Against the backdrop of this immense struggle between the grace and expectations of God's covenant making and the idolatrous wanderings of God's covenant people came a surprising letter from Jeremiah to the Jewish exiles. After exhorting them to build homes, cultivate gardens, and enlarge their families through birth and marriage, the God of Israel said: "But seek the welfare of the city where I have sent you into exile, and pray to the Lord

---

1. Grenz, *Created for Community*, 38.

on its behalf, for in its welfare you will find your welfare."[2] This pronouncement is certainly a statement regarding the necessity of waiting for redemption and return. Yet the exiles are being encouraged to see their captivity as an opportunity to bless their captors; their own wellbeing somehow dependent upon the wellbeing of their host nation, albeit a pagan one. This same letter offers them hope for the future. As always, prophetic words of judgment contained a sense of courage for the present as well as anticipation for the ultimate salvation.

Some of the most direct biblical instructions regarding the church's relationship to governing powers come from the hands of Paul and Peter.[3] Accordingly, it is God who establishes all governmental authority. Christ's followers should, therefore, submit to those authorities willingly and for the Lord's sake. Governors and kings are put in place to punish those who do wrong; these persons have reason to fear. These same rulers are in place to commend those who do right; thus they have no reason to be afraid of ruling authorities. Respect everyone, even the king, and pay taxes. By doing so, Christ's followers silence critics and give a faithful witness to the world.

Paul gives further instruction that it is right to intercede on behalf of kings and other leaders in positions of authority.[4] These directives highlight the need for the church to be proactive in its attitudes and actions toward worldly governmental powers. They stop short, however, of suggesting that the values and narratives of those entities be given a platform within the life of the church for shaping the affections and actions of the church. The right to that influence is reserved by the Father, to be accomplished through Christ by Holy Spirit.

To be sure, not all governing authorities and their leaders act in accord with moral or even legal standards. Yet to the

---

2. Jer 29:7.
3. Rom 13:1–7 and 1 Pet 2:13–17 respectively.
4. 1 Tim 2:1–2.

extent Christ's followers can live in a manner consistent with the prophetic and instructive messages of Jeremiah, Peter, and Paul without breaking biblical principles they should certainly do so. It is biblical to contribute to the common good of life on the earth, certainly a practice engaged in by persons of many faith traditions or even persons who hold no particular religious convictions. It is necessary to remember, however, that what is perceived as the common good by the world in general is by and large short-lived. The whims and fluctuations of the world's settled arrangements mitigate against a world-born eternal peace. Whatever common good can be achieved between the inauguration of God's kingdom in Christ and the coming fullness of God's reign in Christ is, at best, penultimate.

Cultural engagement is an "enduring problem" compounded by the fact that culture is generally considered to be the process and result of human activity.[5] Much is at stake for the church based on its conceptualization of how Christ (and as a result, Christ's followers) relates to human-formed, and thus worldly, cultures. Does the church oppose culture, or does it resonate with the culture? Which determines the terms for engagement, culture or church? How might the church speak to the culture without validating the mores of human culture? Are such distinctions imperative? In response to the latter question, the answer must be "yes," since the hazards are considerable if, in response to the prior three, human culture is accepted *carte blanche* as an appropriate vehicle for the gospel.

An inquiry as to whether some cultures may be more effectual for expressions of the gospel than others may then seem reasonable. A persuasive verdict on this matter is fraught with risk regardless of how sensible the conclusion may seem. The gospel of Jesus has endured in cultures in every corner of the globe throughout the history of the church; it has even prospered in many. Evidence is that the Church may exhibit even greater faithfulness to the gospel

5. Niebuhr, *Christ and Culture*, 32, 40.

in nations and cultures that are antithetical to its message than in those that appear hospitable or supportive of the gospel. Cultures that welcome the gospel openly rarely do so on the gospel's terms, however, preferring their own wisdom as to the true meaning and purpose of the gospel as a message of God's kingdom revealed in and through Jesus Christ.

The ambiguity of human culture is legend. Not all persons within a culture—any culture—experience that culture the same way. Ethnic, gender, and socio-economic biases will vary offering wildly differentiated experiences within that culture. Pluralism and multiculturalism make matters even less simple, and recent trends toward transnational globalism create unique complications that cannot be ignored. Examples of flagrant cultural oppression are exponentially numerous since virtually all human cultures have acted coercively, repressively, or even brutally toward others.

The long-standing principle of niche marketing is deeply ingrained in the American cultural and social psyche. While it is generally benign and rarely demeaning or oppressive, it has nonetheless left its mark on the church in U.S. It is an appealing proposition since "birds of a feather flock together" as the old saying goes. Homogeneity certainly creates momentum for communication, identity, and influence. Little thought is given to how culturally-defined distinctions become divisions. They are ubiquitous in everyday life, perceived as perfectly normal in the broader culture. That such practices seem so sensible to the world is all the more reason for the church to be wary. So long as the church accommodates itself to worldly activities dispersing people across artificial barriers, its witness may be dulled rather than fully expressed.

As noted above, all cultural, economic, ethnic, and social barriers are transcended in Christ. If so, how then will local congregations live out a viable witness to the gospel in ways that are faithful to this dramatic reordering of relationships? One essential dimension of the glory that should come to the triune God through the church as Christ's body globally and locally is the outworking of a tangible, visible, supernaturally shaped unity that transcends all barriers. While certainly not a simple task, the creation of congregations capable of unifying Christians of diverse social, cultural, and racial distinctions may be the most biblically transformative sign of God's kingdom the church can offer the world in the twenty-first century.[6] This is the most challenging work of the gospel facing the church: to enculturate the gospel faithfully while actively standing against worldly practices endemic within various cultures—to be in the world without being of the world.

Therefore, pronouncements that any specific human culture is superior to others for expressing the gospel must be viewed with great concern. It is precisely such determinations that produce cultural triumphalism and entangle *missio Dei* with agendas that are not *missio Dei*. Predicaments of this sort are ideal breeding grounds for nationalism and other potentially idolatrous practices for the church.

Various scripts of human culture may therefore exert their influence upon the church's worship with less than faithful results. Attempts by the church to sustain any worldly culture will likely require liturgical legitimation for the worldly political status quo that contains that culture, a practice that bears the likelihood of reducing Christ to the rank of cultural hero. Any view that values worldly culture as the primary means through which the gospel is communicated to humankind—as opposed to the will and activity of the triune God—tends to overlook the impermanent nature of human culture. Such impermanence may validate secularity within the church, denying the claims of holy God, and allowing various

---

6. Resources by scholar-practitioners that address various dimensions of this task include: *People of the Dream: Multiracial Congregations in the United States* by Michael O. Emerson (Princeton University Press, 2008), *Many Colors: Cultural Intelligence for a Changing Church* by Soong-Chan Rah (Moody Publishers, 2010), *The Color of Church: A Biblical and Practical Paradigm for Multiracial Churches* by Rodney M. Woo (B&H Academic, 2009), and *Building a Healthy Multi-ethnic Church: Mandate, Commitments and Practices of a Diverse Congregation* by Mark DeYmaz (Jossey-Bass, 2007).

contemporaneous cultural forms (including the arts) to become a rival religion. Worship within such an adversarial religion may claim self-righteousness and refute the reality of sin even within the midst of the faith community.[7]

All cultures exist by virtue of ritual actions including language, symbols, behaviors, and gestures by which they enact their concepts of shared uniqueness. The potency of such ritual actions is measured in part by the ability of each culture to differentiate itself from other cultures. The vitality of such differentiation, or lack of it, will influence a culture's ability to thrive or its deterioration. It could be successfully argued that *ekklesia*, the faith community of Christ-followers, is a contradictory culture, existing within yet divergent from all other human cultures. Hence the church expresses the prototype culture of the reign of God in Christ—already begun, yet still emerging.

The metanarrative of empire presupposes the right of empire to its own version of the beginning, unfolding, and ultimate meaning of history (or at least its own place in history). It asserts that right by cultural, political, and economic hegemony; it maintains that hegemony by all means including force, if necessary. To the extent that it can maintain that hegemony, empire can sustain its existence. The creation and maintenance of that hegemony is the project of nationalism.

When the church participates in nationalism, it creates confusion for itself, and indeed the world, regarding the trajectory of history. In biblical terms, reference might be made to the concept of Eschaton. While that term is not likely in common usage in the world at large, the kinds of questions that might lead to eschatological thinking certainly are. What does the future hold for the world and the people who live in it? Will life in the world be better in the future than it is right now? Can the world as it is known today even survive on its current historical path? Is life as it is known in this world all there is to life at all?

7. Wainright, *Doxology*, 390–394.

Commonly described as an understanding of the last things or end times, Eschaton can also refer to the time beginning with Jesus moving toward the culmination of the current age with the full revelation of the reign of God.[8] The ultimate meaning, particularly as viewed through the lens of Revelation, has less to do with chronological history than it does with the in-breaking of God's reign.[9] As witnesses to the kingdom-infused life, teachings, and ministry of Jesus, the gospel accounts of Matthew, Mark, Luke, and John are just as surely eschatological as is the Revelation to John. Luke's record of the birth of the church and initial spread of the gospel of Christ, along with the epistles of Paul and Peter and the writer of the book of Hebrews are profuse with eschatological meaning. Christ's followers who live out the gospel as a kingdom now-kingdom come reality will do so by virtue of faithfulness to eschatologically-shaped worship practices.

A nation-state, in its impulse for self-preservation, will honor growth and even expansion of its population, territory, resources, and influence in service of that self-preservation. It is not likely that a nation-state will accept a view of the future that includes its demise. Nationalism will always, therefore, reject a biblical eschatology since that will mean the end of the empire as the social, cultural, spiritual, and political paradigms of the world acquiesce to the reign of God in Christ.

The identity-making character of worship, reinforced by the theological and political side-taking inherent in worship, makes the church's faithfulness in worship critical for *Missio Dei*. That also makes the church's worship an appealing platform for the world and the world's political machinations toward its own survival. To the extent that the Church responds with any measure of favor toward the world's desires for collaboration, the church will participate in agendas that conflict with rather than support *missio Dei*.

8. Bruce and Scott, "Eschatology," 386.

9. Fiorenza, *Revelation*, 46.

Epilogue

There is no doubt the United States of America is a fortunate nation. Founded by persons determined to create a government unlike any in history, it exists by the sheer will and determination of people who participate in a system that encourages debate and allows dissent. The dynamic tension created by the interplay of freedom and restraint in all realms of life is unique. Democratic capitalism as practiced by the U.S. is by no means perfect, yet there is much to commend life in this system.

Virtually all nationalistically motivated political activity has as its goal the efficient operation and effective survival of the nation-state. That is just as true in the U.S. as in any other nation. Such activity must at times, and in defense of its own system, oppose ideologies that are antithetical to that goal. As with all other nation-states, the propensity to draw on any means necessary to accomplish that goal has meant that the church and its message have always been held close to America's heart. Such attention always creates a moment of truth for Christ's followers, since *missio Dei* will ultimately come into conflict with the agenda of any and all worldly nations—including that of the United States.

For all its goodness, America can be a perilous place for the gospel. While it is ostensibly hospitable to the message of the church, that very hospitality begs vigilance on the part of Christ's followers. The peril exists due to the all-too-easy and frequent blurring of the distinctions between faith and nationalistic fervor rather than from any overt threat by sources within the nation itself.

As noted above, the version of God accepted within the broad American cultural milieu is ambiguous at best in light of the God known through the story of ancient Israel and in the person of Jesus Christ. Whatever ties America may seem to hold to the gospel are defined by America's agenda, not by the mission of the gospel. The demands of the triune God for exclusivity are not met well within America's civil religious environment.

Epilogue

This book has not focused primarily on the nature of America or how America relates to the church and the church's message. Rather the focus has been on the church's perception of itself within the American context, and particularly so in its communal worship among evangelicals. Christ's followers who live in the U.S. should certainly be grateful and acknowledge the values of life in such a society. Yet Christ's followers as the church must be cautious and reject the political *modus operandi* of the U.S. as a means of faithfulness in worship and participation in *missio Dei*.

For reasons outlined above, the task of configuring the consciousness of evangelical Christians to comprehend the politics of Jesus as transcendent over all other worldly political activity is formidable. It is a task that nonetheless must be undertaken. The incorporation of national symbols, themes, and celebrations into the church's worship is strongly ingrained into many corners of the American ecclesial psyche. The danger is explicit however: such practices tend to reinforce the nation's agenda and highlight ways in which America is different from, and even better than, all other nations. Rather, faithful worship will do more to cause Christ's followers to understand the ways in which collectively they are distinct from all other nations on earth—including the United States. Radical faithfulness for the church means refusing to be "influenced [or] intimidated by the values of American culture."[10] The challenge is to foster a living faith among Christ's followers who are able to live as resident aliens—*in*, but not *of* the U.S.

The church has already received all that is necessary for faithful worship from God's Word in Christ. Yet many congregations on the American scene have allowed other agendas to impinge upon their doxological practices. In fact, the church in the U.S. has of its own accord in many places allowed its host nation-state "to skirmish on the church's liturgical turf."[11] Worldly nationalistic impulses inevitably tread on contending ideologies, whether within

10. Manning, *The Signature of Jesus*, 41.
11. Peters, "Worship Wars," 166.

the nation itself or in relation to other nation-states. Just as inevitably, participation in such skirmishes will diminish the church's loyalty to God and *missio Dei*. The result will be a marginalization of the church's metanarrative and seminal acts of worship within ecclesial observances. The fault does not lie with the nation-state; only the church can yield space on its "liturgical turf" allowing the nation-state such opportunity. Only the church can guard its liturgical space; it is not the job of the nation-state to do so. Therefore, the place where the Church must begin to reclaim its identity as alternative *polis* to the American milieu is within its worship.

Like its Jewish forebears the church in all times and in all places has been engaged in a war over worship—between that which is idolatrous and that which is faithful to the one true holy God. Nationalism in the church's worship will inescapably result in idolatry. Such an assertion will understandably produce conflict, not merely between the church and nation but even—and maybe especially—within the church itself. Yet faithfulness in following Christ and announcing the coming reign of God requires that such idolatry be named and cast off.

A grasp of the true political practices of God's reign turns on the response to one question: Does the triune God have authority to claim absolute sovereignty over all dominions? Followers of Christ must answer that question with a resounding "yes" if they are going to be faithful. Yet the church has functioned, in many cases, in ways that appear to answer that question with a confident "yes, but . . . ." In practical ways, the church has denied God's sovereignty over politics by relegating politics to the world, either by immersing itself in the politics of worldly social configurations such as the U.S., or by attempting to abstain from political activity arguing it has no business within that sphere.

If the church believes that God is sovereign over all dominions, it cannot abdicate its role as a political entity and it cannot leave politics solely to worldly entities. It must determine its politics carefully, however. Unless the church's expression of the gospel stands as a clear critique of and contradiction to all worldly social configurations—including that of the U.S.—the result will be a "tragic distortion of the gospel" wherein Jesus' words "are reinterpreted to mean anything, everything, and nothing."[12]

While the gospel of Christ—the good news of the kingdom— is enculturated in specific times and places throughout human history, the operation of this already-but-not-yet-fully-come kingdom resists triumphalist attempts to accomplish that coming via worldly means. The inauguration of that kingdom in Christ was not the work of human wisdom or will, but was accomplished at the bidding of the Father. So too will be the commencement of the fullness of God's reign in Christ, not as the work of human will or wisdom. The kingdom of God will be attained solely by the will of the Father, accomplished through Christ, by the power of Holy Spirit.

Though imperfectly practiced by yet imperfect people, the reign of God is present in the world, though impartially, in the presence of the faith community of Christ-followers known as *ekklesia*—the church. Living the reign of God into reality in a broken and self-preserving world is a commanding task, yet one that is worthy of the highest loyalty to all dimensions of that reign—political as well as social, spiritual, physical, intellectual, and economic.

Faithful worship is a theological vocation for the people of God. Faithful worship has political implications. To the extent that worship challenges the hegemony of worldly socio-economic, gender, and ethnic patterns by positing the politics of the reign of God, it causes the church to fulfill its prophetic task *in the world*. To the extent that worship holds exclusively to the holiness of the triune God of Scripture and avoids the idolatrous claims of all other gods, the church is able to fulfill its prophetic task without being *of the world*.

---

12. Manning, *The Signature of Jesus*, 73.

Because of God's presence by Holy Spirit in the church, the church's communal character precedes and survives the gathering of the body. Regardless of the church's faithfulness to its coming together, if the church is not sent just as faithfully, its communal worship is for naught. The exclusivity with which Christ's followers attend to the triune God in its worship is juxtaposed with its sense of inclusivity in calling non-followers into this worship. *Ekklesia* risks its participation in *missio Dei* when it ignores the full implications of "the graced rhythm of gathering and scattering."[13] One always inclines Christ's followers toward the other. The church is no less the church when it is scattered rather than gathered, and it is no more the church at worship when it is gathered than when it is scattered. In like manner the liturgical practices of God's chosen people who are collectively a holy nation and royal priesthood reveal the reign of God in Christ in all times and all places—gathered or scattered.

Worship must be lived out beyond the gathering of the church. It must be expressed in multiple tangible ways that give evidence of the grace and sovereignty of God in Christ by Holy Spirit. Worship that fails to do that is worship denied. Faithful worship causes the church to exist in the present and as a hope for the future—for the eternal glory of God and for the sake of the world's ultimate redemption.

13. Saliers, *Worship and Spirituality*, 32.

Bibliography

Bacevich, Andrew J. *American Empire: The Realities & Consequences of U.S. Diplomacy.* Cambridge: Harvard University Press, 2002.

Barth, Karl. *Church Dogmatics*, volume IV, The Doctrine of Reconciliation. Translated by G.T. Thomson. Edinburgh: T. & T. Clark, 1962.

Bartley, Jonathan. *Subversive Manifesto: Lifting the Lid on God's Political Agenda.* Oxford:Bible Reading Fellowship. 2003.

Bauckham, Richard. *The Theology of the Book of Revelation.* New York: Cambridge University Press, 1993.

Baxter, Michael J. "God is Not an American: Or, Why Christians Should Not Pledge Allegiance to 'One Nation Under God.'" In *God is Not Religious, Nice, "One of Us," an American, or a Capitalist.* Edited by Brent D. Laytham. Grand Rapids: Brazos, 2004.

Bellah, Robert N. *Beyond Belief: Essays on Religion in a Post-Traditionalist World.* Berkley: University of California Press, 1991.

Benedict XVI (Ratzinger, John). *Jesus of Nazareth: From the Baptism in the Jordan to the Transfiguration.* San Francisco: Ignatius, 2008.

Berger, Peter L., and Richard John Neuhaus. *Against the World for the World: The Hartford Appeal and the Future of American Religion.* New York: Seabury, 1976.

Best, Harold M. *Unceasing Worship: Biblical Perspectives on Worship and the Arts.* Downers Grove IL: InterVarsity, 2003.

Beveridge, Albert J."In Support of an American Empire," 56th Congress, 1st Session, *Congressional Record.* Vol. 33, 705, 711 (January 9, 1900). Online: http://www.thisnation.com/library/beveridge1900.html.

Bock, Darrell L. *Baker Exegetical Commentary on the New Testament: Luke* Volume 2: 9:51—24:53, Third Printing. Edited by Moisés Silva. Grand Rapids: Baker, 2000.

Brewer, David J. *The United States: A Christian Nation.* Philadelphia: The John C. Winston Co., 1905.

Brown, Peter. *The Rise of Western Christendom: Triumph and Diversity, AD 200–1000.* Oxford: Blackwell, 2003.

Bruce, F. F. and J. J. Scott, Jr. "Eschatology," in *The Evangelical Dictionary of Theology.* Edited by Walter A. Elwell. Grand Rapids: Baker Academic, 2001.

Bibliography

Brueggemann, Walter. *Worship in Ancient Israel: An Essential Guide.* Nashville: Abingdon, 2005.

Budde, Michael L. "Selling America, Restricting the Church." In *Anxious About Empire: Theological Essays on the New Global Realities.* Edited by Wes Avram. Grand Rapids: Brazos, 2004.

Bush, George W. "The President's Address to the Nation." (September 12, 2002). Online: http://usinfo.state.gov/usa/s091102.htm.

Butin, Philip W. *The Trinity.* Louisville: Geneva, 2001.

Carson, D.A. "Matthew." In *The Zondervan NIV Bible Commentary, Volume 2: New Testament.* Edited by Kenneth J. Barker and John R. Kohlenberger III. Grand Rapids: Zondervan, 1994.

Carter, Stephen L. *God's Name in Vain: The Wrongs and Rights of Religion in Politics.* New York: Basic, 2000.

———. *The Culture of Disbelief: How American Law and Politics Trivialize Religious Devotion.* New York: Anchor, 1994.

Cavanaugh, William T. "God is Not Religious." In *God is Not . . . : Religious, Nice, "One of Us," An American, A Capitalist.* Edited by D. Brent Latham. Grand Rapids: Brazos Press, 2004.

———. *Theopolitical Imagination: Discovering the Liturgy as a Political Act in an Age of Global Consumerism.* New York: T & T Clark, 2004.

Chapman, Stephen G. "Imperial Exegesis: When Caesar Interprets Scripture." In *Anxious About Empire: Theological Essays on the New Global Realities.* Edited by Wes Aram et al. Grand Rapids: Brazos, 2004.

Clapp, Rodney. *A Peculiar People: The Church as Culture in a Post-Christian Society.* Downers Grove IL: InterVarsity, 1996.

———. "Practicing the Politics of Jesus" In *The Church as Counterculture.* Edited by Michael L. Budde and Robert W. Brimlow. Albany: State University of New York Press, 2000.

Cline, Austin. "America a Christian Nation—Is the United States a Christian Nation?" About.com. Online: http://atheism.about.com/od/americachristiannation/a/AmericaChristianNation.htm.

Cyril of Alexandria, *Commentary on the Gospel of St. Luke.* Translated by R. Payne Smith. Long Island: Studion, 1983.

Dawn, Marva J. *A Royal "Waste" of Time: The Splendor of Worshiping God and Being Church for the World.* Grand Rapids: Eerdmans, 1999.

———. *How Shall We Worship? Biblical Guidelines for the Worship Wars.* Wheaton: Tyndale House, 2003.

———. *Powers, Weakness, and the Tabernacling of God.* Grand Rapids: Eerdmans, 2001.

———. *Reaching Out Without Dumbing Down: A Theology of Worship for the Turn-of-the-Century Culture.* Grand Rapids: Eerdmans, 1995.

Drane, John. *The McDonaldization of the Church: Spirituality, Creativity, and the Future of the Church.* London: Darton, Longman and Todd, 2005.

Dykstra, Craig, and Dorothy C. Bass. "A Theological Understanding of Christian Practices." In *Practicing Theology: Beliefs and Practices in Christian Life.* Edited by Miroslav Volf and Dorothy C. Bass. Grand Rapids: Eerdmans, 2002.

Eidsmoe, John. "Obama: America Not a Christian Nation." New American, 15 April 2009. Online: http://www.thenewamerican.com/usnews/election/1003.

Fiorenza, Elisabeth Schüssler. *Revelation: Vision of a Just World.* Minneapolis MI: Fortress, 1991.

Gedicks, Frederick M. "The Religious, the Secular, and the Antithetical." *Capital University Law Review* 20, 1991.

Graham, Fred W. *The Constructive Revolutionary: John Calvin and His Socio-Economic Impact.* Atlanta: John Knox Press, 1971.

Green, Joel B. "The Gospel of Luke." In *The New International Commentary on the New Testament.* Edited by Gordon D. Fee. Grand Rapids: Eerdmans, 1997.

Grenz, Stanley J. *Created for Community: Connecting Christian Belief with Christian Living,* Second Edition. Grand Rapids: Baker, 2000.

Guder, Darrell L., Editor et al. *Missional Church: A Vision for the Sending of the Church in North America.* Grand Rapids: Eerdmans, 1998.

Gunton, Colin. *The Promise of Trinitarian Theology,* Second Edition. Edinburgh: T & T Clark, 1997.

Hall, Douglas John. *The End of Christendom and the Future of Christianity.* Eugene, OR: Wipf and Stock, 2002.

Harvey, Barry A. *Another City: An Ecclesiological Primer for a Post-Christian World.* Harrisburg, PA: Trinity Press International, 1999.

Hauerwas, Stanley M., and William H. Willimon. *Resident Aliens: Life in the Christian Colony.* Nashville: Abingdon, 1989.

Herbert, David. *Religion and Civil Society: Rethinking Public Religion in the Contemporary World.* London: Ashgate, 2003.

Hewell, Rob. "Faithful Worship." In *The Minister's Manual: The Minister's Complete Sourcebook,* 2010 Edition. Edited by Lee McGlone. San Francisco: Jossey-Bass, 2010.

Horsley, Richard A. *Jesus and Empire: The Kingdom of God and the New World Disorder.* Minneapolis MI: Fortress, 2003.

———. *Religion and Empire: People, Power, and the Life of the Spirit.* Minneapolis, MI: Fortress Press, 2003.

Howard-Brook, Wes and Anthony Gwyther. *Unveiling Empire: Reading Revelation Then and Now.* Maryknoll, NY: Orbis, 1999.

Bibliography

Hurtado, Larry W. *At the Origins of Christian Worship: The Context and Character of Earliest Christian Devotion.* Grand Rapids: Eerdmans, 1999.

Kenneson, Philip D., and James L. Street. *Selling Out the Church: The Dangers of Church Marketing.* Eugene, OR: Cascade, 2003.

Lebacqz, Karen. *Word, Worship, World, & Wonder: Reflections on Christian Living.* Nashville: Abingdon, 1997.

Manning, Brennan. *The Signature of Jesus.* Sisters, OR: Multnomah, 1996.

Marshall, I. Howard. "Luke." In *New Bible Commentary: 21st Century Edition.* Edited by G.J. Wenham et al. Leicester, UK: InterVarsity, 1994.

May, Henry F. *The Enlightenment in America.* New York: Oxford University Press, 1976.

Meeks, M. Douglas. *God the Economist: The Doctrine of God and Political Economy.* Minneapolis MI: Fortress, 1989.

Murray, Stuart. *Post-Christendom: Church and Mission in a Strange New World.* Carlisle, U.K.: Paternoster, 2004.

Newbigin, Lesslie. *Foolishness to the Greeks: The Gospel and Western Culture.* Grand Rapids: Eerdmans, 1986.

———. *The Gospel in a Pluralist Society.* Grand Rapids: Eerdmans, 1989.

Niebuhr, H. Richard. *Christ and Culture.* New York: Harper, 1956.

Noll, Mark A. *America's God: From Jonathan Edwards to Abraham Lincoln.* New York: Oxford University Press, 2002.

———. *One Nation Under God? Christian Faith & Political Action in America.* San Francisco: Harper & Row, 1988.

Novak, Michael. *The Spirit of Democratic Capitalism.* Lanham, MD.: Madison, 1991.

Origen, "Exposition Continued: the King and the Servants." *Commentary on the Gospel of Matthew.* Translated by John Patrick. Online: http://mbsoft .com/believe/txua/origenmu.htm.

Osborn, Robert T. *The Barmen Declaration as a Paradigm for a Theology of the American Church.* Lewiston, NY: Mellen, 1991.

Peters, Ted. "Worship Wars." In *Dialog,* 33:3, 1994.

Peterson, Eugene H. *Subversive Spirituality.* Grand Rapids: Eerdmans, 1997.

Plantinga Jr., Cornelius. *Not the Way It's Supposed to Be: A Breviary of Sin.* Grand Rapids: Eerdmans, 1995.

Poulton, John. *People Under Pressure.* London: Lutterworth, 1973.

Reagan, Ronald. "Remarks at the Annual Convention of the National Association of Evangelicals in Orlando, Florida, March 8, 1983" (1983). Online: http: //www.reagan.utexas.edu/archives/speeches/1983/30883b.htm.

Rowley, H.H. *Worship in Ancient Israel: Its Forms and Meaning.* London: SPCK, 1967.

Saliers, Don E. *Worship and Spirituality* Second Edition. Akron OH: Order of Saint Luke, 1996.

Sawyer, Mary R. *The Church on the Margins: Living Christian Community.* Harrisburg, PA: Trinity Press International, 2003.

Schmemann, Alexander. *For the Life of the World*, rev. ed. Crestwood, NY: St. Vladimir's, 1973.

Smith, Christian, and Melinda Lundquist Denton. *Soul Searching: The Religious & Spiritual Lives of American Teenagers.* New York: Oxford University Press, 2005.

Snyder, Howard A. *Liberating the Church: The Ecology of Church & Kingdom.* Downers Grove IL: InterVarsity, 1983.

Storkey, Alan. *Jesus and Politics: Confronting the Powers.* Grand Rapids: Baker Academic, 2005.

Thorne, Mister. "The Tangled Web of Ceremonial Deism." In *Liberty Magazine* (September–October 2003). Online: from http://www.libertymagazine .org/index.php?id=1204.

Wainwright, Geoffrey. *Doxology: The Praise of God in Worship, Doctrine, and Life.* New York: Oxford University Press, 1980.

Walls, Andrew F. *The Missionary Movement in Christian History: Studies in the Transmission of Faith*, Tenth Printing. Maryknoll, NY: Orbis, 2005.

Walsh, Brian J. and Sylvia C. Keesmaat. *Colossians Remixed: Subverting the Empire.* Grand Rapids: IVP Academic, 2004.

Wannenwetsch, Bernd. *Political Worship: Ethics for Christian Citizens.* Translated by Margaret Kohl. New York: Oxford University Press, 2004

Webber, Robert E., and Rodney Clapp. *People of the Truth: The Power of the Worshiping Community in the Modern World.* Eugene, OR: Wipf and Stock, 2001.

Willimon, William H. *The Intrusive Word: Preaching to the Unbaptized.* Nashville: Abingdon, 1994.

Wink, Walter. *The Powers that Be: Theology for a New Millennium.* New York: Galilee Doubleday, 1998.

Witherington, Ben. *Matthew.* Macon, GA: Smyth & Helwys, 2006.

Wright, N.T. *For All God's Worth: True Worship and the Calling of the Church.* Grand Rapids: Eerdmans, 1997.

———. *Surprised by Hope: Rethinking Heaven, the Resurrection, and the Mission of the Church.* New York: HarperOne, 2008.

Yoder, John Howard. *Body Politics: Five Practices of the Christian Community Before the Watching World.* Scottdale, PA: Herald, 2001.

———. *For the Nations: Essays Evangelical and Public.* Eugene, OR: Wipf and Stock, 2002.

———. *He Came Preaching Peace.* Scottdale, PA: Herald, 1985.

———. *The Original Revolution.* Scottdale, PA: Herald, 1977.

Made in the USA
Columbia, SC
13 August 2018